The Search for the Biblical Jesus

JON F. DEWEY

WESTBOW
PRESS
A DIVISION OF THOMAS NELSON

Unless otherwise indicated, Bible quotations are taken from the King James Version of the Bible.

WestBow Press books may be ordered through booksellers or by contacting:

WestBow Press
A Division of Thomas Nelson
1663 Liberty Drive
Bloomington, IN 47403
www.westbowpress.com
1-(866) 928-1240

ISBN: 978-1-4497-3478-7 (hc)
ISBN: 978-1-4497-3477-0 (sc)
ISBN: 978-1-4497-3476-3 (e)

Library of Congress Control Number: 2011962756

Printed in the United States of America

WestBow Press rev. date: 1/10/2012

INTRODUCTION

I started writing this in the 1990s after hearing about the work of the Jesus Seminar and their book "The Five Gospels." In their book, the Seminar was attempting to discover the real sayings of Jesus by voting on which passages they thought were *not* authentic sayings. Their finding was to dismiss the majority of the gospel sayings (including the entire book of John) as inauthentic or forgeries. Their conclusions really disturbed me. I started this book as a response because when I read the gospels, I did not come to the same outcome they did. My conclusions were quite the opposite.

Unfortunately, life and a military career took over as priorities, and this book was literally put on the shelf. But thanks to the release of the Mel Gibson movie "The Passion of the Christ" and Dan Brown's "The DaVinci Code" there was a renewal of interest in the person of Jesus Christ, who he is, and how the biblical documentation of his life affects us today. While there has been a renewal of research into who Jesus was historically, unfortunately the conclusions once again are against the gospel records. Attempts are made to discredit or redefine who Jesus was and why he was here. It seems like scholarship is against the Bible and the gospels and against Jesus in particular. I decided that what I once had to say on this subject was very valid and very necessary as an opposing viewpoint. What was popularly being presented motivated me to pull out the manuscript and complete it.

What I find most unsettling about the Jesus Seminar, and other modern scholarship, is that for their research to be absolutely true, then there is no basis for Christianity to stand on. If the gospels are not true, if Jesus was a myth or the fabrication of someone later in history, then we have a tremendous problem. One of the bedrock doctrines of Christianity is the work of Jesus himself. His death on the cross paid the penalty for our sins and his triumph over death at the Resurrection enables us to have eternal life. If these events did not occur then millions of people died believing a lie, and we are hopelessly lost. As the Apostle Paul said:

> "But if there be no resurrection of the dead, then is Christ not risen:
> And if Christ be not risen, then is our preaching vain, and your faith is also vain.
> For if the dead rise not, then is not Christ raised:
> And if Christ be not raised, your faith is vain; ye are yet in your sins.
> Then they also which are fallen asleep in Christ are perished.
> If in this life only we have hope in Christ, we are of all men most miserable."
> (1 Corinthians 15:13-14, 16-19)

If the gospel message is not true then we are still separated from God and there is no hope. If the gospel message is not true then as believers in Jesus Christ we are foolish. We have chosen to live a disciplined and austere life in order to receive a reward in heaven, rather than living for pleasure here. If the gospel is not true then we are wasting our time and depriving ourselves for nothing. Life is meaningless and we might as well fall into despair.

But if the gospel message is true then we have reason for hope. Christ died to bring us back into right relationship with God. Life is not meaningless because we have our ultimate purpose in our relationship with our Creator.

What I would like to attempt to do in this book is look at the gospel record and discover what it has to say for and about itself. In doing so, I am looking at three specific areas:

a. What does Jesus say about himself as being God (or the Son of God), about himself as being here to save the lost, and that salvation is only through him?

b. What do others say about him being God, and the Messiah?
c. What evidence does the Bible itself give that point to Jesus being God, the Messiah of Israel, and the Savior of mankind?

The specific gospel book I will use is the book of John. I fully realize that this book is considered a complete forgery by the Jesus Seminar. I have not chosen it because it was rejected by them. On the contrary, I chose it because it is familiar to most Christians and non-Christians alike, and is traditionally a book which is accepted as showing Jesus as Messiah.

Everyone who enters into the discussion of who Jesus is inevitably does so with certain personal presuppositions. While many researchers and writers state they are looking for "truth," it appears to me that they have decided upon the end state, or the answer they wanted in the first place, and then make the evidence fit their conclusion. Unfortunately, this is possible to do when interpreting Scripture. It is especially easy to get away with this method in our modern society where very few people have read the gospel message for themselves. The usual outcome is that Jesus is dismissed as being just another prophet or as being a good guy whose life story the apostles later manipulated to further their own religious or political goals. Because of these negative presuppositions, the gospel accounts are concluded to be riddled with errors or to be outright forgeries. The reader is left with conclusions that neither reflect traditional orthodox beliefs nor are accurate by biblical standards.

I, too, approach the subject with presuppositions. They are more in line with traditionally held beliefs, and are mainly these two:

a. I believe that the Scriptures as we have them are the inspired and unique Word of God. I make no apologies about this. I am an evangelical, born again believer in Jesus Christ. I believe the evidence points that it is reasonable to accept the traditional claims of Christianity: Jesus is who the gospels say he was, that he lived historically as written, and that he died paying the penalty for our sins on the cross.
b. Each person should read the source texts and make up their minds themselves. Religious faith is far too important of a

matter to be left in the hands of scholars. Laymen are just as capable of making theological discoveries as anyone. This is why there has been, and still continues to be, such a thrust to place the Scriptures into the hands of people in their own native language. The gospel message is for every-day people, not just clergy or academics. For that reason I have included word-for-word the entire gospel of John. Do not take someone else's word for it. Read the actual text. Then make up your own mind.

I do not pretend to think that my book is the last word on the subject of Jesus' divinity. It is not exhaustive, and in some ways it is not complete due to time and other restrictions. This book is the presentation of my ideas into a discussion that has been ongoing for thousands of years. Like in any discussion, you are free to accept or reject any opinion I am offering.

THE GOSPEL OF JOHN

CHAPTER 1

1 In the beginning was the Word, and the Word was with God, and the Word was God.
2 The same was in the beginning with God.
3 All things were made by him; and without him was not any thing made that was made.
4 In him was life; and the life was the light of men.
5 And the light shineth in darkness; and the darkness comprehended it not.

The gospel of John opens with what is considered to be the definitive statement about who Jesus is and was and will always be: deity. "The Word" was a concept used in Greek philosophy. The Greek translated "Word" is *Logos*, the Infinite Idea, the consciousness that brought all consciousness into being.

John is writing to an audience who immediately understood those concepts. This opening statement parallels the introduction in the book of Genesis and the creation story. John describes Jesus as being the one who created all things, the original active idea. He is not a separate entity but uniquely the deity we call God. John hints here at the Trinity also. Jesus is revealed to be the creative part of the Trinity, the one who spoke and the heavens and earth were created.

6 There was a man sent from God, whose name was John.
7 The same came for a witness, to bear witness of the Light, that all men through him might believe.

8 He was not that Light, but was sent to bear witness of that Light.
9 That was the true Light, which lighteth every man that cometh into the world.

This section describes Jesus' mission to come to the earth and to bring spiritual light to a dark and fallen world. This passage is another reference to the divine nature of Jesus, calling him the *true Light*. Jesus is the only one who can give illumination and understanding to people. This concept of Jesus coming to bring light and redemption was not an idea invented by John the Apostle. John the Baptist was giving this same witness of Jesus' coming *before* he had officially met him in the gospel record.

10 He was in the world, and the world was made by him, and the world knew him not.
11 He came unto his own, and his own received him not.
12 But as many as received him, to them gave he power to become the sons of God, even to them that believe on his name:
13 Which were born, not of blood, nor of the will of the flesh, nor of the will of man, but of God.
14 And the Word was made flesh, and dwelt among us, (and we beheld his glory, the glory as of the only begotten of the Father,) full of grace and truth.

This is a very clear statement that Jesus is the Redeemer and Messiah, and that salvation is only through him. While this passage asserts that Jesus was rejected by the Jewish nation of his time, the offer of forgiveness and salvation is granted now to *anyone* who believes in him.

In this passage John reemphasizes that Jesus is the *Logos*, and that he was recognized by his disciples as being God in the flesh. He is *the only begotten of the Father*. No other person in history is entitled to be called by that name.

15 John bare witness of him, and cried, saying, This was he of whom I spake, He that cometh after me is preferred before me: for he was before me.
16 And of his fulness have all we received, and grace for grace.
17 For the law was given by Moses, but grace and truth came by Jesus Christ.
18 No man hath seen God at any time; the only begotten Son, which is in the bosom of the Father, he hath declared him.

The message of John the Baptist to the people is a testimony to the deity of the Messiah. While the Messiah would physically arrive on the scene after John had started his ministry, this person would have existed before John was ever born. Jesus is again called *the only begotten Son*, who lives in *the bosom of the Father*, signifying that he is uniquely God.

19 And this is the record of John, when the Jews sent priests and Levites from Jerusalem to ask him, Who art thou?
20 And he confessed, and denied not; but confessed, I am not the Christ.
21 And they asked him, What then? Art thou Elias? And he saith, I am not. Art thou that prophet? And he answered, No.
22 Then said they unto him, Who art thou? that we may give an answer to them that sent us. What sayest thou of thyself?
23 He said, I am the voice of one crying in the wilderness, Make straight the way of the Lord, as said the prophet Esaias.
24 And they which were sent were of the Pharisees.
25 And they asked him, and said unto him, Why baptizest thou then, if thou be not that Christ, nor Elias, neither that prophet?
26 John answered them, saying, I baptize with water: but there standeth one among you, whom ye know not;
27 He it is, who coming after me is preferred before me, whose shoe's latchet I am not worthy to unloose.
28 These things were done in Bethabara beyond Jordan, where John was baptizing.

John the Baptist clearly knew what his mission was: to proclaim the coming of the Messiah. He reemphasizes that the person who will follow after him will be of higher status that himself. The reference to not being worthy to unloose this person's shoe shows John's opinion of the vast difference in status and worth between himself and the one who was to come. John understood that he was the forerunner of the Messiah. This understanding is disclosed by his identifying himself as the fulfillment of Isaiah 40:3:

> *The voice of him that crieth in the wilderness, Prepare ye the way of the LORD, make straight in the desert a highway for our God.*

"That prophet" is a reference to a prediction made by Moses. Moses predicted that God would send another prophet like himself who would lead Israel. The identity of this prophet is Jesus of Nazareth, the Messiah. Moses' pronouncement about this future prophet is found in Deuteronomy 18:15-19:

> *15 The LORD thy God will raise up unto thee a Prophet from the midst of thee, of thy brethren, like unto me; unto him ye shall harken;*
> *16 According to all that thou desiredst of the LORD thy God in Horeb in the day of the assembly, saying, Let me not hear again the voice of the LORD my God, neither let me see this great fire any more, that I die not.*
> *17 And the LORD said unto me, They have well spoken that which they have spoken.*
> *18 I will raise them up a Prophet from among their brethren, like unto thee, and will put my words in his mouth; and he shall speak unto them all that I shall command him.*
> *19 And it shall come to pass, that whosoever will not hearken unto my words which he shall speak in my name, I will require it of him.*

> *29 The next day John seeth Jesus coming unto him, and saith, Behold the Lamb of God, which taketh away the sin of the world.*
> *30 This is he of whom I said, After me cometh a man which is preferred before me: for he was before me.*

31 And I knew him not: but that he should be made manifest to Israel, therefore am I come baptizing with water.
32 And John bare record, saying, I saw the Spirit descending from heaven like a dove, and it abode upon him.
33 And I knew him not: but he that sent me to baptize with water, the same said unto me, Upon whom thou shalt see the Spirit descending, and remaining on him, the same is he which baptizeth with the Holy Ghost.
34 And I saw, and bare record that this is the Son of God.

When John finally does meet Jesus, he immediately recognizes him and gives public recognition to Jesus as the coming Messiah. John points directly at Jesus and speaks in metaphors that would not be lost on the people. By calling Jesus the Lamb of God who would take away the sins of the world, John identified Jesus with the peace-offering given on the people's behalf. John is clearly identifying Jesus as the Redeemer of humanity, the one who will bring peace and reconciliation between sinful man and righteous God.

John the Baptist's vision of the Holy Spirit descending on Jesus was a fulfillment of a previous message given to him by God. John was told that the person who would receive the Holy Spirit would be the one he was preparing the way for. This person would baptize with the Holy Spirit, an attribute that identifies the person as deity because only God can give His Spirit.

35 Again the next day after John stood, and two of his disciples;
36 And looking upon Jesus as he walked, he saith, Behold the Lamb of God!
37 And the two disciples heard him speak, and they followed Jesus.
38 Then Jesus turned, and saw them following, and saith unto them, What seek ye? They said unto him, Rabbi, (which is to say, being interpreted, Master,) where dwellest thou?
39 He saith unto them, Come and see. They came and saw where he dwelt, and abode with him that day: for it was about the tenth hour.

In this passage, John the Baptist again states that Jesus is the peace-offering lamb foreshadowed in Leviticus Chapter Three. This comment is not lost on two of John's disciples, who immediately turn to Jesus and start to follow him.

40 One of the two which heard John speak, and followed him, was Andrew, Simon Peter's brother.
41 He first findeth his own brother Simon, and saith unto him, We have found the Messias, which is, being interpreted, the Christ.
42 And he brought him to Jesus. And when Jesus beheld him, he said, Thou art Simon the son of Jona: thou shalt be called Cephas, which is by interpretation, A stone.

Andrew, originally a follower of John the Baptist, turns and begins to follow Jesus based on John's testimony about him. Andrew is so convinced that Jesus is the prophesied Messiah that he tells his brother Peter and brings Peter to personally meet him. This is a life changing event for Peter, because he not only follows Jesus, but receives a pronouncement and prediction about his later influence in the birth of the church.

43 The day following Jesus would go forth into Galilee, and findeth Philip, and saith unto him, Follow me.
44 Now Philip was of Bethsaida, the city of Andrew and Peter.
45 Philip findeth Nathanael, and saith unto him, We have found him, of whom Moses in the law, and the prophets, did write, Jesus of Nazareth, the son of Joseph.
46 And Nathanael said unto him, Can there any good thing come out of Nazareth? Philip saith unto him, Come and see.
47 Jesus saw Nathanael coming to him, and saith of him, Behold an Israelite indeed, in whom is no guile!
48 Nathanael saith unto him, Whence knowest thou me? Jesus answered and said unto him, Before that Philip called thee, when thou wast under the fig tree, I saw thee.
49 Nathanael answered and saith unto him, Rabbi, thou art the Son of God; thou art the King of Israel.

50 Jesus answered and said unto him, Because I said unto thee, I saw thee under the fig tree, believest thou? thou shalt see greater things than these.

51 And he saith unto him, Verily, verily, I say unto you, Hereafter ye shall see heaven open, and the angels of God ascending and descending upon the Son of man.

Jesus' impact on people was phenomenal. Immediately after meeting Jesus, Phillip not only followed him but also believed he was the Messiah. Philip told his friend Nathanael about Jesus, identifying him as the promised Messiah prophesied in the Old Testament. Nathanael was skeptical, but on meeting Jesus he too was convinced.

CHAPTER 2

1 And the third day there was a marriage in Cana of Galilee; and the mother of Jesus was there:
2 And both Jesus was called, and his disciples, to the marriage.
3 And when they wanted wine, the mother of Jesus saith unto him, They have no wine.
4 Jesus saith unto her, Woman, what have I to do with thee? mine hour is not yet come.
5 His mother saith unto the servants, Whatsoever he saith unto you, do it.

This incident illustrates the belief that Mary had in her own son. She had absolute confidence that he could provide what was needed. Mary's instructions to the servants showed how completely she believed that Jesus could (and would) perform this miracle. This is testimony from Mary that Jesus was the Messiah, the Son of God.

6 And there were set there six waterpots of stone, after the manner of the purifying of the Jews, containing two or three firkins apiece.
7 Jesus saith unto them, Fill the waterpots with water. And they filled them up to the brim.
8 And he saith unto them, Draw out now, and bear unto the governor of the feast. And they bare it.
9 When the ruler of the feast had tasted the water that was made wine, and knew not whence it was: (but the servants which drew the water knew;) the governor of the feast called the bridegroom,

10 And saith unto him, Every man at the beginning doth set forth good wine; and when men have well drunk, then that which is worse; but thou hast kept the good wine until now.
11 This beginning of miracles did Jesus in Cana of Galilee, and manifested forth his glory; and his disciples believed on him.

Miracles are one of the proofs the Apostle John gives to show that Jesus is the Messiah and the Son of God. Unlike our modern misunderstanding of miracles, in the gospels they are not for show or personal gain of any kind. They have a threefold purpose: to demonstrate that the God of Israel is the true God and deity, to verify that Scripture is the Word of God, and as evidence that Jesus is the Messiah. Miracles are never performed "on demand" but for specific reasons. This is Jesus' first miracle to show people that he is the awaited Messiah.

12 After this he went down to Capernaum, he, and his mother, and his brethren, and his disciples: and they continued there not many days.
13 And the Jews' passover was at hand, and Jesus went up to Jerusalem,
14 And found in the temple those that sold oxen and sheep and doves, and the changers of money sitting:
15 And when he had made a scourge of small cords, he drove them all out of the temple, and the sheep, and the oxen; and poured out the changers' money, and overthrew the tables;
16 And said unto them that sold doves, Take these things hence; make not my Father's house an house of merchandise.
17 And his disciples remembered that it was written, The zeal of thine house hath eaten me up.

In this passage, Jesus makes a statement with serious implications. Jesus calls the Temple "my Father's house." The Temple is the dwelling place of God on earth. Jesus identifies the God of the Temple and his Father as the same person. By identifying God as his Father in this way, Jesus is clearly stating he is deity.

18 Then answered the Jews and said unto him, What sign shewest thou unto us, seeing that thou doest these things?
19 Jesus answered and said unto them, Destroy this temple, and in three days I will raise it up.
20 Then said the Jews, Forty and six years was this temple in building, and wilt thou rear it up in three days?
21 But he spake of the temple of his body.
22 When therefore he was risen from the dead, his disciples remembered that he had said this unto them; and they believed the scripture, and the word which Jesus had said.

The religious leaders were not happy with Jesus running the merchants out of the temple. Immediately they challenged him, demanding to see some kind of credentials of authority for upsetting the status quo. The answer Jesus gave apparently confused them. Jesus' proof of his divine authority would be his resurrection from the dead. Later, the disciples remembered this statement and realized that Jesus was making a prophecy about himself. Jesus' resurrection would be the ultimate testimony of his deity.

23 Now when he was in Jerusalem at the passover, in the feast day, many believed in his name, when they saw the miracles which he did.
24 But Jesus did not commit himself unto them, because he knew all men,
25 And needed not that any should testify of man: for he knew what was in man.

After seeing Jesus perform miracles, more people believed that Jesus was the Messiah. John again emphasizes that miracles are one of the credentials required for someone to be recognized as the Messiah. Jesus more than met this qualification.

CHAPTER 3

1 There was a man of the Pharisees, named Nicodemus, a ruler of the Jews:

2 The same came to Jesus by night, and said unto him, Rabbi, we know that thou art a teacher come from God: for no man can do these miracles that thou doest, except God be with him.

3 Jesus answered and said unto him, Verily, verily, I say unto thee, Except a man be born again, he cannot see the kingdom of God.

4 Nicodemus saith unto him, How can a man be born when he is old? can he enter the second time into his mother's womb, and be born?

5 Jesus answered, Verily, verily, I say unto thee, Except a man be born of water and of the Spirit, he cannot enter into the kingdom of God.

6 That which is born of the flesh is flesh; and that which is born of the Spirit is spirit.

7 Marvel not that I said unto thee, Ye must be born again.

8 The wind bloweth where it listeth, and thou hearest the sound thereof, but canst not tell whence it cometh, and whither it goeth: so is every one that is born of the Spirit.

9 Nicodemus answered and said unto him, How can these things be?

10 Jesus answered and said unto him, Art thou a master of Israel, and knowest not these things?

11 Verily, verily, I say unto thee, We speak that we do know, and testify that we have seen; and ye receive not our witness.

12 If I have told you earthly things, and ye believe not, how shall ye believe, if I tell you of heavenly things?

13 And no man hath ascended up to heaven, but he that came down from heaven, even the Son of man which is in heaven.

14 And as Moses lifted up the serpent in the wilderness, even so must the Son of man be lifted up:
15 That whosoever believeth in him should not perish, but have eternal life.

In this famous passage of the conversation between Jesus and Nicodemus, Jesus several times referred to his divinity. In verse 11, Jesus makes a stunning change of pronoun, changing from "I" to "We." Jesus is clearly identifying himself with God, using the language of Genesis 1:26-27:

26 And God said, Let us make man in our image, after our likeness: and let them have dominion over the fish of the sea, and over the fowl of the air, and over the cattle, and over all the earth, and over every creeping thing that creepeth upon the earth.
27 So God created man in his own image, in the image of God created he him; male and female created he them.

John shows through his own words how Jesus, the *Logos*, was there at the creation and identifies him as the active part of the Trinity during the act of creation.

Jesus made several other statements to Nicodemus concerning his Godhood. In verse 13, Jesus testifies that his origins are supernatural. He, the Son of man, came down from heaven, which is his place of origin. No *man* has ever been there, but *he* has. This clearly shows His divinity.

16 For God so loved the world, that he gave his only begotten Son, that whosoever believeth in him should not perish, but have everlasting life.
17 For God sent not his Son into the world to condemn the world; but that the world through him might be saved.
18 He that believeth on him is not condemned: but he that believeth not is condemned already, because he hath not believed in the name of the only begotten Son of God.

Most "red-letter" Bibles identify these verses as being spoken by Jesus. The more I have read this passage over the years, the more I am convinced that these are the words of John the author. Either way, in this passage Jesus is called God's Son, which shows his relationship to God the Father and his divine nature. Jesus is clearly shown as the only vehicle by which the world and individuals can be saved from judgment and condemnation.

19 And this is the condemnation, that light is come into the world, and men loved darkness rather than light, because their deeds were evil.

20 For every one that doeth evil hateth the light, neither cometh to the light, lest his deeds should be reproved.

21 But he that doeth truth cometh to the light, that his deeds may be made manifest, that they are wrought in God.

In this passage the author assumes that Jesus is uniquely God, and not just a normal man. He is sent from God and is equal to the God of the Old Testament. This passage may also be commenting on the errors of the Gnostics by identifying Jesus as *the light* that men must come to in order to be on the path to God (as opposed to the false illumination of Gnostic mysticism). Anyone who opposes *the light* is not more spiritual but is in the darkness and doing evil.

22 After these things came Jesus and his disciples into the land of Judaea; and there he tarried with them, and baptized.

23 And John also was baptizing in Aenon near to Salim, because there was much water there: and they came, and were baptized.

24 For John was not yet cast into prison.

25 Then there arose a question between some of John's disciples and the Jews about purifying.

26 And they came unto John, and said unto him, Rabbi, he that was with thee beyond Jordan, to whom thou barest witness, behold, the same baptizeth, and all men come to him.

27 John answered and said, A man can receive nothing, except it be given him from heaven.

28 Ye yourselves bear me witness, that I said, I am not the Christ, but that I am sent before him.
29 He that hath the bride is the bridegroom: but the friend of the bridegroom, which standeth and heareth him, rejoiceth greatly because of the bridegroom's voice: this my joy therefore is fulfilled.
30 He must increase, but I must decrease.

In this lengthy passage John the Baptist several times testifies that Jesus is the coming Messiah and divine. Jesus is shown as the Christ, the bridegroom, and not from this world but coming from heaven. John reinforces to his followers that he is simply the messenger and not the coming King they are looking for. Unfortunately, it appears that his disciples are either rather slow to get this point or purposely deciding to stay with John. They admitted that John pointed out Jesus as the Messiah but they were still with him. The oddity of this whole situation is that they were complaining about Jesus gaining a bigger crowd than John had! John had to correct them. It was Jesus who was the main event, not him.

31 He that cometh from above is above all: he that is of the earth is earthly, and speaketh of the earth: he that cometh from heaven is above all.
32 And what he hath seen and heard, that he testifieth; and no man receiveth his testimony.
33 He that hath received his testimony hath set to his seal that God is true.
34 For he whom God hath sent speaketh the words of God: for God giveth not the Spirit by measure unto him.
35 The Father loveth the Son, and hath given all things into his hand.
36 He that believeth on the Son hath everlasting life: and he that believeth not the Son shall not see life; but the wrath of God abideth on him.

John in this passage again testifies to Jesus' divinity. Jesus, because he is of heavenly origin, has greater knowledge and experience than any ordinary man. Jesus came from God, was sent by God, speaks the words of God, and has the Holy Spirit without limit. The only way that he could have all those attributes is to be part of the Godhead himself.

CHAPTER 4

1 When therefore the Lord knew how the Pharisees had heard that Jesus made and baptized more disciples than John,
2 (Though Jesus himself baptized not, but his disciples,)
3 He left Judaea, and departed again into Galilee.
4 And he must needs go through Samaria.
5 Then cometh he to a city of Samaria, which is called Sychar, near to the parcel of ground that Jacob gave to his son Joseph.
6 Now Jacob's well was there. Jesus therefore, being wearied with his journey, sat thus on the well: and it was about the sixth hour.
7 There cometh a woman of Samaria to draw water: Jesus saith unto her, Give me to drink.
8 (For his disciples were gone away unto the city to buy meat.)
9 Then saith the woman of Samaria unto him, How is it that thou, being a Jew, askest drink of me, which am a woman of Samaria? for the Jews have no dealings with the Samaritans.
10 Jesus answered and said unto her, If thou knewest the gift of God, and who it is that saith to thee, Give me to drink; thou wouldest have asked of him, and he would have given thee living water.

After entering into this conversation with the woman at the well, Jesus got right to the point of who he is. Jesus testified to her about himself as being God, because only God can give the Holy Spirit.

11 The woman saith unto him, Sir, thou hast nothing to draw with, and the well is deep: from whence then hast thou that living water?

12 Art thou greater than our father Jacob, which gave us the well, and drank thereof himself, and his children, and his cattle?
13 Jesus answered and said unto her, Whosoever drinketh of this water shall thirst again:
14 But whosoever drinketh of the water that I shall give him shall never thirst; but the water that I shall give him shall be in him a well of water springing up into everlasting life.
15 The woman saith unto him, Sir, give me this water, that I thirst not, neither come hither to draw.
16 Jesus saith unto her, Go, call thy husband, and come hither.
17 The woman answered and said, I have no husband. Jesus said unto her, Thou hast well said, I have no husband:
18 For thou hast had five husbands; and he whom thou now hast is not thy husband: in that saidst thou truly.
19 The woman saith unto him, Sir, I perceive that thou art a prophet.

Even after Jesus was more direct with her about who he was than he had been with most people, she still did not understand who he was. While Jesus was speaking of spiritual concepts using everyday items as illustrations, she thought he was talking about everyday earthly things. In verse 14 Jesus again referred to the Holy Spirit and the life the Spirit can give, but she still did not understand. It was only after Jesus confronted her with her personal secrets, things he could not have humanly known, that she began to understand that the person she was talking to was not just an ordinary Jewish man.

20 Our fathers worshipped in this mountain; and ye say, that in Jerusalem is the place where men ought to worship.
21 Jesus saith unto her, Woman, believe me, the hour cometh, when ye shall neither in this mountain, nor yet at Jerusalem, worship the Father.
22 Ye worship ye know not what: we know what we worship: for salvation is of the Jews.
23 But the hour cometh, and now is, when the true worshippers shall worship the Father in spirit and in truth: for the Father seeketh such to worship him.

24 God is a Spirit: and they that worship him must worship him in spirit and in truth.
25 The woman saith unto him, I know that Messias cometh, which is called Christ: when he is come, he will tell us all things.
26 Jesus saith unto her, I that speak unto thee am he.

Jesus continued to walk the woman through this conversation, until she brought up the subject of the Messiah. In one of the clearest passages in the gospels, Jesus plainly states that he is the Messiah that she was referring to. Passages such as this one dispel any notion that Jesus did not think he was the Messiah or Son of God.

27 And upon this came his disciples, and marvelled that he talked with the woman: yet no man said, What seekest thou? or, Why talkest thou with her?
28 The woman then left her waterpot, and went her way into the city, and saith to the men,
29 Come, see a man, which told me all things that ever I did: is not this the Christ?
30 Then they went out of the city, and came unto him.

The woman at the well understood completely what Jesus was saying. She was so utterly convinced that Jesus was the coming Messiah that she left what she was doing and went back into her city, testifying in public about him.

31 In the mean while his disciples prayed him, saying, Master, eat.
32 But he said unto them, I have meat to eat that ye know not of.
33 Therefore said the disciples one to another, Hath any man brought him ought to eat?
34 Jesus saith unto them, My meat is to do the will of him that sent me, and to finish his work.
35 Say not ye, There are yet four months, and then cometh harvest? behold, I say unto you, Lift up your eyes, and look on the fields; for they are white already to harvest.

36 And he that reapeth receiveth wages, and gathereth fruit unto life eternal: that both he that soweth and he that reapeth may rejoice together.
37 And herein is that saying true, One soweth, and another reapeth.
38 I sent you to reap that whereon ye bestowed no labour: other men laboured, and ye are entered into their labours.

In verse 34 Jesus reminds his disciples that he has been sent by God, and that he is on a specific mission from God.

39 And many of the Samaritans of that city believed on him for the saying of the woman, which testified, He told me all that ever I did.
40 So when the Samaritans were come unto him, they besought him that he would tarry with them: and he abode there two days.
41 And many more believed because of his own word;
42 And said unto the woman, Now we believe, not because of thy saying: for we have heard him ourselves, and know that this is indeed the Christ, the Saviour of the world.

The people, who lived in the town, after hearing what the woman who was at the well said about Jesus, came out to hear for themselves. What is often overlooked in this story is that Jesus stayed with them for two days teaching and preaching. These people heard Jesus' teaching firsthand and believed what he had to say. Their own testimony is that Jesus is the Messiah, the Savior and the Son of God.

43 Now after two days he departed thence, and went into Galilee.
44 For Jesus himself testified, that a prophet hath no honour in his own country.
45 Then when he was come into Galilee, the Galilaeans received him, having seen all the things that he did at Jerusalem at the feast: for they also went unto the feast.
46 So Jesus came again into Cana of Galilee, where he made the water wine. And there was a certain nobleman, whose son was sick at Capernaum.

47 When he heard that Jesus was come out of Judaea into Galilee, he went unto him, and besought him that he would come down, and heal his son: for he was at the point of death.
48 Then said Jesus unto him, Except ye see signs and wonders, ye will not believe.
49 The nobleman saith unto him, Sir, come down ere my child die.
50 Jesus saith unto him, Go thy way; thy son liveth. And the man believed the word that Jesus had spoken unto him, and he went his way.
51 And as he was now going down, his servants met him, and told him, saying, Thy son liveth.
52 Then enquired he of them the hour when he began to amend. And they said unto him, Yesterday at the seventh hour the fever left him.
53 So the father knew that it was at the same hour, in the which Jesus said unto him, Thy son liveth: and himself believed, and his whole house.
54 This is again the second miracle that Jesus did, when he was come out of Judaea into Galilee.

While this passage makes Jesus sound like he is stern and a bit cruel, he is really showing another aspect of his credentials as Messiah and God. The use of miracles was a proof that he is who he claimed to be, but he did not want people coming to him simply because they wanted to see a show. He questioned the sincerity and motives of the nobleman who came to him. Satisfied that the man's faith was real, Jesus then healed his child. It is important to note that this miracle demonstrated the depth of Jesus' power over sickness and human infirmity. Unlike previous miracles, this one was performed from a distance. Jesus did not have to be present to heal or perform miracles. He performed them because it was his will to do so. The end result was exactly what the miracles were there for: the nobleman and his family believed that Jesus was the Messiah, the Son of God.

CHAPTER 5

1 After this there was a feast of the Jews; and Jesus went up to Jerusalem.

2 Now there is at Jerusalem by the sheep market a pool, which is called in the Hebrew tongue Bethesda, having five porches.

3 In these lay a great multitude of impotent folk, of blind, halt, withered, waiting for the moving of the water.

4 For an angel went down at a certain season into the pool, and troubled the water: whosoever then first after the troubling of the water stepped in was made whole of whatsoever disease he had.

5 And a certain man was there, which had an infirmity thirty and eight years.

6 When Jesus saw him lie, and knew that he had been now a long time in that case, he saith unto him, Wilt thou be made whole?

7 The impotent man answered him, Sir, I have no man, when the water is troubled, to put me into the pool: but while I am coming, another steppeth down before me.

8 Jesus saith unto him, Rise, take up thy bed, and walk.

9 And immediately the man was made whole, and took up his bed, and walked: and on the same day was the sabbath.

In this passage Jesus publicly displayed by use of a miracle that he is the Messiah, the Son of God. Jesus has full authority over physical ailments. What I find interesting about the conversation between Jesus and the man is how much it is real life. The man was incapacitated for thirty-eight years. Jesus asked him if he wanted to be healed, but instead of saying yes, the man replied instead that he was unable to get into the pool. This is how we are: we as humans are so often fixated on the mechanics of how something should happen that we miss it when the opportunity comes to have what we want in the first place. Jesus did not ask if the man wanted to get into the pool, he asked if he wanted to be healed!

10 The Jews therefore said unto him that was cured, It is the sabbath day: it is not lawful for thee to carry thy bed.
11 He answered them, He that made me whole, the same said unto me, Take up thy bed, and walk.
12 Then asked they him, What man is that which said unto thee, Take up thy bed, and walk?
13 And he that was healed wist not who it was: for Jesus had conveyed himself away, a multitude being in that place.
14 Afterward Jesus findeth him in the temple, and said unto him, Behold, thou art made whole: sin no more, lest a worse thing come unto thee.
15 The man departed, and told the Jews that it was Jesus, which had made him whole.

This illustrates the omnipotent power that Jesus has. He did not need for the man to know who he was or to believe anything about him. Jesus healed this man simply because he wanted to.

16 And therefore did the Jews persecute Jesus, and sought to slay him, because he had done these things on the sabbath day.

A common theme throughout all four gospels is the reactions of the Jewish leaders. Jesus performed some of his miracles specifically to show the religious leaders the correct interpretation of the Mosaic law. Instead of using the teachings of the law to point the way to God, they made men slaves to the law, and specifically to their strict Sabbath interpretations and observations. Jesus in his actions and teachings was showing them the actual purpose of the Old Testament law.

17 But Jesus answered them, My Father worketh hitherto, and I work.

18 Therefore the Jews sought the more to kill him, because he not only had broken the sabbath, but said also that God was his Father, making himself equal with God.

This passage is another one where Jesus very clearly identifies that he is deity. This was so clear that the religious leaders wanted to take action against him because he claimed equality with God.

19 Then answered Jesus and said unto them, Verily, verily, I say unto you, The Son can do nothing of himself, but what he seeth the Father do: for what things soever he doeth, these also doeth the Son likewise.
20 For the Father loveth the Son, and sheweth him all things that himself doeth: and he will shew him greater works than these, that ye may marvel.
21 For as the Father raiseth up the dead, and quickeneth them; even so the Son quickeneth whom he will.
22 For the Father judgeth no man, but hath committed all judgment unto the Son:
23 That all men should honour the Son, even as they honour the Father. He that honoureth not the Son honoureth not the Father which hath sent him.

In this set of verses, Jesus is again plainly pronouncing his total equality with God. Jesus completely identified himself as *the Son*. He is talking about himself here, not some shadowy figure yet to be revealed. *The Father* is deity, God himself. By identifying specific miraculous and powerful acts that only the Father can do, and ascribing them equally to the Son, Jesus is point blank saying that he is equal to God the Father, and has the same authority as God the Father. The identification of the Son as being equal with the Father demands the conclusion that the Son, Jesus, is deity himself.

24 Verily, verily, I say unto you, He that heareth my word, and believeth on him that sent me, hath everlasting life, and shall not come into condemnation; but is passed from death unto life.

25 Verily, verily, I say unto you, The hour is coming, and now is, when the dead shall hear the voice of the Son of God: and they that hear shall live.
26 For as the Father hath life in himself; so hath he given to the Son to have life in himself;
27 And hath given him authority to execute judgment also, because he is the Son of man.
28 Marvel not at this: for the hour is coming, in the which all that are in the graves shall hear his voice,
29 And shall come forth; they that have done good, unto the resurrection of life; and they that have done evil, unto the resurrection of damnation.

This passage continues Jesus' revelation of himself as having equality with God, and that he is deity. Jesus claims for himself attributes that in the Old Testament law were exclusive attributes of God: the ability to give eternal life, the power to raise the dead back to life and the authority to pass final judgment. Jesus ascribes these abilities to *the Son of God* and *the Son of man*, both terms that were identified earlier as being Jesus himself. All of these are figures the Jewish people at the time would immediately understand. Jesus was also using apocalyptic imagery. He identified himself as the one who will voice the command for the dead to rise, and as the one who will sit in final judgment.

30 I can of mine own self do nothing: as I hear, I judge: and my judgment is just; because I seek not mine own will, but the will of the Father which hath sent me.
31 If I bear witness of myself, my witness is not true.
32 There is another that beareth witness of me; and I know that the witness which he witnesseth of me is true.
33 Ye sent unto John, and he bare witness unto the truth.
34 But I receive not testimony from man: but these things I say, that ye might be saved.
35 He was a burning and a shining light: and ye were willing for a season to rejoice in his light.
36 But I have greater witness than that of John: for the works which the Father hath given me to finish, the same works that I do, bear witness of me, that the Father hath sent me.

37 And the Father himself, which hath sent me, hath borne witness of me. Ye have neither heard his voice at any time, nor seen his shape.
38 And ye have not his word abiding in you: for whom he hath sent, him ye believe not.

To answer the skepticism of the religious leaders, Jesus uses legal images and language. Acknowledging that they may doubt him talking about himself, he goes on to present other witnesses who testify of him as being the Messiah and the Son of God. First Jesus points to John the Baptist. John verbally testified to them who Jesus was. Jesus then takes the level of reliability up several notches. He explains to them that as trustworthy as John's testimony is, it is God the Father himself who gives the ultimate testimony. The Father's testimony about Jesus is demonstrated by the miracles that the leaders saw and experienced with their own eyes. The testimony from the miracles is indisputable evidence of Jesus' divinity.

39 Search the scriptures; for in them ye think ye have eternal life: and they are they which testify of me.
40 And ye will not come to me, that ye might have life.
41 I receive not honour from men.
42 But I know you, that ye have not the love of God in you.
43 I am come in my Father's name, and ye receive me not: if another shall come in his own name, him ye will receive.
44 How can ye believe, which receive honour one of another, and seek not the honour that cometh from God only?
45 Do not think that I will accuse you to the Father: there is one that accuseth you, even Moses in whom ye trust.
46 For had ye believed Moses, ye would have believed me: for he wrote of me.
47 But if ye believe not his writings, how shall ye believe my words?

Another unimpeachable testimony as to who Jesus was came from the Old Testament scriptures. Jesus points out to the religious leaders that the very scriptures they claim to believe gave all the evidence they needed to know that he is the Son of God.

CHAPTER 6

1 After these things Jesus went over the sea of Galilee, which is the sea of Tiberias.

2 And a great multitude followed him, because they saw his miracles which he did on them that were diseased.

3 And Jesus went up into a mountain, and there he sat with his disciples.

4 And the passover, a feast of the Jews, was nigh.

5 When Jesus then lifted up his eyes, and saw a great company come unto him, he saith unto Philip, Whence shall we buy bread, that these may eat?

6 And this he said to prove him: for he himself knew what he would do.

7 Philip answered him, Two hundred pennyworth of bread is not sufficient for them, that every one of them may take a little.

8 One of his disciples, Andrew, Simon Peter's brother, saith unto him,

9 There is a lad here, which hath five barley loaves, and two small fishes: but what are they among so many?

10 And Jesus said, Make the men sit down. Now there was much grass in the place. So the men sat down, in number about five thousand.

11 And Jesus took the loaves; and when he had given thanks, he distributed to the disciples, and the disciples to them that were set down; and likewise of the fishes as much as they would.

12 When they were filled, he said unto his disciples, Gather up the fragments that remain, that nothing be lost.

13 Therefore they gathered them together, and filled twelve baskets with the fragments of the five barley loaves, which remained over and above unto them that had eaten.

The incident with the loaves and fishes is a miracle showing his kingship over the human condition, and his ability to meet human needs.

14 Then those men, when they had seen the miracle that Jesus did, said, This is of a truth that prophet that should come into the world. 15 When Jesus therefore perceived that they would come and take him by force, to make him a king, he departed again into a mountain himself alone.

After the miraculous feeding of multitude, many of those who were following Jesus became convinced he was the Messiah. They wanted to take him and make him king of Israel by acclamation. The mob wanted a conquering Messiah who would overthrow the Roman occupation and reestablish the Davidic throne in Jerusalem. Jesus' mission on earth was not to be a conquering warrior, but to be obedient to God and to die on the cross as the sacrifice for the sins of humanity. The phrase *that prophet* again refers to the passage in Deuteronomy where Moses points out that there will be another prophet who will be like him, except greater.

16 And when even was now come, his disciples went down unto the sea, 17 And entered into a ship, and went over the sea toward Capernaum. And it was now dark, and Jesus was not come to them. 18 And the sea arose by reason of a great wind that blew. 19 So when they had rowed about five and twenty or thirty furlongs, they see Jesus walking on the sea, and drawing nigh unto the ship: and they were afraid. 20 But he saith unto them, It is I; be not afraid. 21 Then they willingly received him into the ship: and immediately the ship was at the land whither they went.

Jesus here shows his kingly and divine authority over nature. Jesus' power extends over nature even to the point of the very molecules in the water. He commands them to be solid and walks across them in defiance of the laws of nature.

22 The day following, when the people which stood on the other side of the sea saw that there was none other boat there, save that one whereinto his disciples were entered, and that Jesus went not with his disciples into the boat, but that his disciples were gone away alone;

23 (Howbeit there came other boats from Tiberias nigh unto the place where they did eat bread, after that the Lord had given thanks:)

24 When the people therefore saw that Jesus was not there, neither his disciples, they also took shipping, and came to Capernaum, seeking for Jesus.

25 And when they had found him on the other side of the sea, they said unto him, Rabbi, when camest thou hither?

26 Jesus answered them and said, Verily, verily, I say unto you, Ye seek me, not because ye saw the miracles, but because ye did eat of the loaves, and were filled.

27 Labour not for the meat which perisheth, but for that meat which endureth unto everlasting life, which the Son of man shall give unto you: for him hath God the Father sealed.

28 Then said they unto him, What shall we do, that we might work the works of God?

29 Jesus answered and said unto them, This is the work of God, that ye believe on him whom he hath sent.

30 They said therefore unto him, What sign shewest thou then, that we may see, and believe thee? what dost thou work?

The idea of signs or credentials was not new. The Jewish nation would know exactly who their Messiah was. This person would perform some very specific tasks that would be evidence they could make a conclusion from. Jesus met all the qualifications to be the Messiah.

31 Our fathers did eat manna in the desert; as it is written, He gave them bread from heaven to eat.

32 Then Jesus said unto them, Verily, verily, I say unto you, Moses gave you not that bread from heaven; but my Father giveth you the true bread from heaven.

33 For the bread of God is he which cometh down from heaven, and giveth life unto the world.

The reference to manna in the desert alluded to the Jewish nation during the Exodus and their wandering for forty years. Jesus corrected a misconception that some in the crowd had about the source of the manna. They attributed the manna as being a work of Moses, while Jesus correctly pointed out that the manna was actually from God. He then turned the conversation, and explained that just as manna was from God, so was he. He is the true bread from heaven that gives life.

34 Then said they unto him, Lord, evermore give us this bread.
35 And Jesus said unto them, I am the bread of life: he that cometh to me shall never hunger; and he that believeth on me shall never thirst.
36 But I said unto you, That ye also have seen me, and believe not.

Unfortunately, they did not seem to understand what he was saying. Jesus was not talking about bread like food; he was using figurative language to point out that he was God. Jesus may have been referencing Isaiah 55:1, where God tells the Israelites that he will meet all of their needs:

Ho, every one that thirsteth, come ye to the waters, and he that hath no money; come ye, buy, and eat; yea, come, buy wine and milk without money and without price.

37 All that the Father giveth me shall come to me; and him that cometh to me I will in no wise cast out.
38 For I came down from heaven, not to do mine own will, but the will of him that sent me.
39 And this is the Father's will which hath sent me, that of all which he hath given me I should lose nothing, but should raise it up again at the last day.
40 And this is the will of him that sent me, that every one which seeth the Son, and believeth on him, may have everlasting life: and I will raise him up at the last day.
41 The Jews then murmured at him, because he said, I am the bread which came down from heaven.

42 And they said, Is not this Jesus, the son of Joseph, whose father and mother we know? how is it then that he saith, I came down from heaven?

In this passage, Jesus is speaking about his supernatural beginnings and the mission he came with. Jesus *came down from heaven*, showing his supernatural nature. And like in earlier passages, he takes for himself duties and prerogatives that are ascribed in the Old Testament as being reserved for God himself: the ability to raise people to life on the Day of Judgment and the ability to give to people eternal life if they believe on him. His hearers, of course, did not understand what he was saying. I do not think they believed that Jesus was anyone special. They knew his family. They could not conceive of him having a supernatural origin.

43 Jesus therefore answered and said unto them, Murmur not among yourselves.
44 No man can come to me, except the Father which hath sent me draw him: and I will raise him up at the last day.
45 It is written in the prophets, And they shall be all taught of God. Every man therefore that hath heard, and hath learned of the Father, cometh unto me.

Jesus gives us some insight into how spiritual understanding happens. Someone is drawn to Jesus and believes his message because the Father puts a "spark" of the Holy Spirit into the person that enables the understanding of spiritual things. A person who listens to this drawing from the Father will be able to understand and be able to come to Jesus and see him for who he really is.

46 Not that any man hath seen the Father, save he which is of God, he hath seen the Father.
47 Verily, verily, I say unto you, He that believeth on me hath everlasting life.
48 I am that bread of life.
49 Your fathers did eat manna in the wilderness, and are dead.

50 This is the bread which cometh down from heaven, that a man may eat thereof, and not die.

51 I am the living bread which came down from heaven: if any man eat of this bread, he shall live for ever: and the bread that I will give is my flesh, which I will give for the life of the world.

52 The Jews therefore strove among themselves, saying, How can this man give us his flesh to eat?

53 Then Jesus said unto them, Verily, verily, I say unto you, Except ye eat the flesh of the Son of man, and drink his blood, ye have no life in you.

54 Whoso eateth my flesh, and drinketh my blood, hath eternal life; and I will raise him up at the last day.

55 For my flesh is meat indeed, and my blood is drink indeed.

56 He that eateth my flesh, and drinketh my blood, dwelleth in me, and I in him.

57 As the living Father hath sent me, and I live by the Father: so he that eateth me, even he shall live by me.

58 This is that bread which came down from heaven: not as your fathers did eat manna, and are dead: he that eateth of this bread shall live for ever.

59 These things said he in the synagogue, as he taught in Capernaum.

This passage is one of the bluntest concerning Jesus' claims to divinity. It is very clear: he came from heaven, sent on a mission from God himself (verse 38); he has the ability to give eternal life to the person who believes in him, and has the ability to raise that person on the last day, both abilities that are reserved for God himself (verse 40); his words are the direct teachings of deity (verse 45); he claims that he has seen the Father, but only deity can have that ability (verse 46); and again emphasizes that belief in him gives eternal life, the giving of which is ascribed to God alone (verse 47). Finally, he claims to be the *bread of life*—the substance that came from heaven and grants eternal life.

Jesus compares himself to the manna that the Jewish ancestors ate in the wilderness. While they were sustained on the bread of the manna in the wilderness, they still eventually died. His bread, which is himself, will not only sustain in this existence, but in the next also. Using language that foreshadows his words during the last supper, Jesus proclaims that his body and blood will give eternal life and resurrection on the last day.

60 Many therefore of his disciples, when they had heard this, said, This is an hard saying; who can hear it?

61 When Jesus knew in himself that his disciples murmured at it, he said unto them, Doth this offend you?

62 What and if ye shall see the Son of man ascend up where he was before?

63 It is the spirit that quickeneth; the flesh profiteth nothing: the words that I speak unto you, they are spirit, and they are life.

64 But there are some of you that believe not. For Jesus knew from the beginning who they were that believed not, and who should betray him.

65 And he said, Therefore said I unto you, that no man can come unto me, except it were given unto him of my Father.

66 From that time many of his disciples went back, and walked no more with him.

67 Then said Jesus unto the twelve, Will ye also go away?

68 Then Simon Peter answered him, Lord, to whom shall we go? thou hast the words of eternal life.

69 And we believe and are sure that thou art that Christ, the Son of the living God.

70 Jesus answered them, Have not I chosen you twelve, and one of you is a devil?

71 He spake of Judas Iscariot the son of Simon: for he it was that should betray him, being one of the twelve.

These were pretty advanced concepts for the crowds to hear. They were so difficult that many of them decided that they no longer wanted to follow Jesus. It is almost as if the teachings made them realize that this novelty was harder than they wanted to put effort into. When Jesus questioned those that stayed, Peter makes a spontaneous announcement. He openly declares that Jesus is the Messiah and is the Son of God. Peter claims outright that he believes that Jesus is deity. Jesus never rebukes Peter for saying this, or rejects Peter's open elevation and worship of him.

CHAPTER 7

1 After these things Jesus walked in Galilee: for he would not walk in Jewry, because the Jews sought to kill him.

2 Now the Jews' feast of tabernacles was at hand.

3 His brethren therefore said unto him, Depart hence, and go into Judaea, that thy disciples also may see the works that thou doest.

4 For there is no man that doeth any thing in secret, and he himself seeketh to be known openly. If thou do these things, shew thyself to the world.

5 For neither did his brethren believe in him.

6 Then Jesus said unto them, My time is not yet come: but your time is always ready.

7 The world cannot hate you; but me it hateth, because I testify of it, that the works thereof are evil.

8 Go ye up unto this feast: I go not up yet unto this feast; for my time is not yet full come.

9 When he had said these words unto them, he abode still in Galilee.

10 But when his brethren were gone up, then went he also up unto the feast, not openly, but as it were in secret.

11 Then the Jews sought him at the feast, and said, Where is he?

12 And there was much murmuring among the people concerning him: for some said, He is a good man: others said, Nay; but he deceiveth the people.

13 Howbeit no man spake openly of him for fear of the Jews.

Jesus was rejected and criticized by all sorts of people. Some of his critics appeared to be from his own family. While there is no record of how this rejection affected him, Jesus nevertheless stayed true to the mission he was given by the Father. He was not going to do anything simply to satisfy the selfish wants or curiosity of people. Some of the people who heard the message gave the impression they believed it, however. At the feast there is much discussion about Jesus, but those who had any favoritism toward him were forced to keep it to themselves because of the social pressure exerted by the religious leaders.

14 Now about the midst of the feast Jesus went up into the temple, and taught.

15 And the Jews marvelled, saying, How knoweth this man letters, having never learned?

16 Jesus answered them, and said, My doctrine is not mine, but his that sent me.

17 If any man will do his will, he shall know of the doctrine, whether it be of God, or whether I speak of myself.

18 He that speaketh of himself seeketh his own glory: but he that seeketh his glory that sent him, the same is true, and no unrighteousness is in him.

19 Did not Moses give you the law, and yet none of you keepeth the law? Why go ye about to kill me?

20 The people answered and said, Thou hast a devil: who goeth about to kill thee?

21 Jesus answered and said unto them, I have done one work, and ye all marvel.

22 Moses therefore gave unto you circumcision; (not because it is of Moses, but of the fathers;) and ye on the sabbath day circumcise a man.

23 If a man on the sabbath day receive circumcision, that the law of Moses should not be broken; are ye angry at me, because I have made a man every whit whole on the sabbath day?

24 Judge not according to the appearance, but judge righteous judgment.

25 Then said some of them of Jerusalem, Is not this he, whom they seek to kill?

26 But, lo, he speaketh boldly, and they say nothing unto him. Do the rulers know indeed that this is the very Christ?

27 Howbeit we know this man whence he is: but when Christ cometh, no man knoweth whence he is.

When Jesus did go to the feast he went to the temple and taught the people. What I find amazing is that no one criticized the *content* of Jesus' teachings. They instead criticized *him*. I have found this to be a fairly standard tactic of the world. If you cannot beat the argument . . . then attack the speaker!

Another very common criticism is one of academic credentials. Jesus' teaching is singled out because he never went to the sanctioned schools. This is the same criticism leveled against the apostles in Chapter Four of the book of Acts. If you did not go to the right school, then you do not have the right teaching. Jesus corrects his critics for their false assumption about his teaching by telling them that it did not come from any school, but was taught to him directly from God. (Jesus is again clearly identifying himself as the prophet predicted by Moses in Deuteronomy 18. The message of the prophet that was to come would be directly from God. The significance of this statement could not have been missed by the religious leaders.)

Based on the evidence they were seeing the regular people started to wonder if Jesus really could be the Messiah. They have their doubts about who Jesus is but they know that the Messiah will come performing signs exactly like the ones they were witnessing.

28 Then cried Jesus in the temple as he taught, saying, Ye both know me, and ye know whence I am: and I am not come of myself, but he that sent me is true, whom ye know not.
29 But I know him: for I am from him, and he hath sent me.
30 Then they sought to take him: but no man laid hands on him, because his hour was not yet come.
31 And many of the people believed on him, and said, When Christ cometh, will he do more miracles than these which this man hath done?
32 The Pharisees heard that the people murmured such things concerning him; and the Pharisees and the chief priests sent officers to take him.

33 Then said Jesus unto them, Yet a little while am I with you, and then I go unto him that sent me.

34 Ye shall seek me, and shall not find me: and where I am, thither ye cannot come.

35 Then said the Jews among themselves, Whither will he go, that we shall not find him? will he go unto the dispersed among the Gentiles, and teach the Gentiles?

36 What manner of saying is this that he said, Ye shall seek me, and shall not find me: and where I am, thither ye cannot come?

Jesus understands the people's internal doubts and answers them. Jesus flatly states he is divinity by claiming to be from God and sent by God. Many in the crowd do start to understand and realize that Jesus is fulfilling prophecy and performing the acts that are the credentials of the Messiah. The Pharisees and other religious leaders unfortunately do not get it. When Jesus speaks of his future return to his heavenly home, they think he is talking about a journey to another part of the empire, and show they are totally confused.

37 In the last day, that great day of the feast, Jesus stood and cried, saying, If any man thirst, let him come unto me, and drink.

38 He that believeth on me, as the scripture hath said, out of his belly shall flow rivers of living water.

39 (But this spake he of the Spirit, which they that believe on him should receive: for the Holy Ghost was not yet given; because that Jesus was not yet glorified.)

40 Many of the people therefore, when they heard this saying, said, Of a truth this is the Prophet.

41 Others said, This is the Christ. But some said, Shall Christ come out of Galilee?

42 Hath not the scripture said, That Christ cometh of the seed of David, and out of the town of Bethlehem, where David was?

43 So there was a division among the people because of him.

Jesus many times used the image of water for the pouring out of the Holy Spirit in fulfillment of Joel 2:28. Jesus may also have been alluding to Jeremiah 2:13. In the passage in Jeremiah God is shown to be the only source of living water. Jesus is again revealing himself to be deity by pointing to himself as the source of living water.

Jesus' teaching was beginning to sink in and many were starting to believe. Unfortunately, instead of investigating more, some formed their judgment of him based on superficial evidence. While Jesus did *live* in the area of Galilee, he was not *born* in the Galilee region. Jesus was born in Bethlehem, fulfilling the prophecy. A person would have to get to know him to know that.

> *44 And some of them would have taken him; but no man laid hands on him.*
> *45 Then came the officers to the chief priests and Pharisees; and they said unto them, Why have ye not brought him?*
> *46 The officers answered, Never man spake like this man.*
> *47 Then answered them the Pharisees, Are ye also deceived?*
> *48 Have any of the rulers or of the Pharisees believed on him?*
> *49 But this people who knoweth not the law are cursed.*
> *50 Nicodemus saith unto them, (he that came to Jesus by night, being one of them,)*
> *51 Doth our law judge any man, before it hear him, and know what he doeth?*
> *52 They answered and said unto him, Art thou also of Galilee? Search, and look: for out of Galilee ariseth no prophet.*
> *53 And every man went unto his own house.*

The religious leaders had this same misunderstanding as the crowds. They did not know where Jesus was actually born, either, and assumed he was born in Galilee. This misunderstanding may have been a factor in their rejection of Jesus as their Messiah.

CHAPTER 8

1 Jesus went unto the mount of Olives.

2 And early in the morning he came again into the temple, and all the people came unto him; and he sat down, and taught them.

3 And the scribes and Pharisees brought unto him a woman taken in adultery; and when they had set her in the midst,

4 They say unto him, Master, this woman was taken in adultery, in the very act.

5 Now Moses in the law commanded us, that such should be stoned: but what sayest thou?

6 This they said, tempting him, that they might have to accuse him. But Jesus stooped down, and with his finger wrote on the ground, as though he heard them not.

7 So when they continued asking him, he lifted up himself, and said unto them, He that is without sin among you, let him first cast a stone at her.

8 And again he stooped down, and wrote on the ground.

9 And they which heard it, being convicted by their own conscience, went out one by one, beginning at the eldest, even unto the last: and Jesus was left alone, and the woman standing in the midst.

10 When Jesus had lifted up himself, and saw none but the woman, he said unto her, Woman, where are those thine accusers? hath no man condemned thee?

11 She said, No man, Lord. And Jesus said unto her, Neither do I condemn thee: go, and sin no more.

In this famous episode called "the woman caught in adultery" or "the woman caught in sin," Jesus is being challenged by the religious leaders over someone they claim was caught in the act. Adultery was a serious charge, one that under the Mosaic law carried a death penalty.

This was another of the seemingly no-win situations that the religious leaders liked to put Jesus in. If he showed compassion and said to release her then he could be accused of breaking the law himself. If he said that they should stone her then they could accuse him of not showing love and for inciting a murder. (To keep this situation in historical context, we have to remember that the Jewish nation did not have the legal ability to execute lawbreakers. This was a right reserved for the Roman government.)

Once again Jesus turned the tables on the religious leaders. Jesus agreed that the law did indeed state that a person caught in adultery should be stoned. He then gave an additional criterion: only the person who was without sin could cast the first stone. The crowd slowly faded away, because they knew that in reality no one is without sin.

Only after the crowd dispersed did Jesus confront the woman. I can imagine that he already knew the condition of her heart. She is humiliated and sorrowful. She is fully aware that she is in sin. At this moment, Jesus offers her compassion, not judgment. Using authority that only God can have, Jesus forgives her and tells her to sin no more. Jesus is also consistent to his own teaching. Being the only person without sin, he has the right to cast a stone. Instead, he opts to not exercise this right but to show mercy.

Jesus' action with the woman also casts light on how we should handle some modern problems. Jesus never once denied the law. He also never denied mercy and compassion. What Jesus did deny to the religious leaders was their over rigid legalism. Jesus never said that the woman's sin was acceptable. What he accepted was the woman herself as a person. This is where we get it wrong in our modern application of biblical principles. Showing mercy and compassion does not mean denying the precepts of the law. And the law does not automatically preclude mercy and compassion. These are not mutually exclusive.

12 Then spake Jesus again unto them, saying, I am the light of the world: he that followeth me shall not walk in darkness, but shall have the light of life.

13 The Pharisees therefore said unto him, Thou bearest record of thyself; thy record is not true.

14 Jesus answered and said unto them, Though I bear record of myself, yet my record is true: for I know whence I came, and whither I go; but ye cannot tell whence I come, and whither I go.

15 Ye judge after the flesh; I judge no man.

16 And yet if I judge, my judgment is true: for I am not alone, but I and the Father that sent me.

17 It is also written in your law, that the testimony of two men is true.

18 I am one that bear witness of myself, and the Father that sent me beareth witness of me.

19 Then said they unto him, Where is thy Father? Jesus answered, Ye neither know me, nor my Father: if ye had known me, ye should have known my Father also.

20 These words spake Jesus in the treasury, as he taught in the temple: and no man laid hands on him; for his hour was not yet come.

As Jesus reveals to the crowds more about his divinity, the Pharisees challenged him saying that whatever he was saying could not be true because he was talking about himself. Jesus countered this rather lame challenge by giving more testimony about him being divine. The Pharisees wanted more witnesses, so Jesus gave them another: The Father himself. If the Pharisees understood anything about Jesus they would have known he was divine and equal to his Father who sent him.

21 Then said Jesus again unto them, I go my way, and ye shall seek me, and shall die in your sins: whither I go, ye cannot come.

22 Then said the Jews, Will he kill himself? because he saith, Whither I go, ye cannot come.

23 And he said unto them, Ye are from beneath; I am from above: ye are of this world; I am not of this world.

24 I said therefore unto you, that ye shall die in your sins: for if ye believe not that I am he, ye shall die in your sins.

25 Then said they unto him, Who art thou? And Jesus saith unto them, Even the same that I said unto you from the beginning.
26 I have many things to say and to judge of you: but he that sent me is true; and I speak to the world those things which I have heard of him.
27 They understood not that he spake to them of the Father.

This excerpt starts a lengthy, seemingly cryptic discussion between Jesus and the crowd around him. I say that it is seemingly cryptic, because it is quite clear if it is understood in the context Jesus presented it. Jesus was speaking about his coming death and resurrection. This could only be understood if taken in the context of Jesus being the Messiah and God. Jesus is very specific in his statements that he is deity: he is *from above*; he is *not of this world*; and *I am he* (meaning the Messiah). These statements apparently confused the crowds, who asked for a clarification. The only clarification Jesus gives is that he is what he has been saying from the beginning: the Messiah, the Son of God.

28 Then said Jesus unto them, When ye have lifted up the Son of man, then shall ye know that I am he, and that I do nothing of myself; but as my Father hath taught me, I speak these things.
29 And he that sent me is with me: the Father hath not left me alone; for I do always those things that please him.
30 As he spake these words, many believed on him.

Jesus reveals to the crowd that after they have him crucified, then some will understand that he is the Messiah, and that he is God.

31 Then said Jesus to those Jews which believed on him, If ye continue in my word, then are ye my disciples indeed;
32 And ye shall know the truth, and the truth shall make you free.

Some of the people in the crowd seemed to understand the message. Jesus turns his attention to them. Jesus explains to them that his teachings point to truth and the truth will always point to him as the Son of God. Knowing the truth about Christ will set you free in many ways.

33 They answered him, We be Abraham's seed, and were never in bondage to any man: how sayest thou, Ye shall be made free?

34 Jesus answered them, Verily, verily, I say unto you, Whosoever committeth sin is the servant of sin.

35 And the servant abideth not in the house for ever: but the Son abideth ever.

36 If the Son therefore shall make you free, ye shall be free indeed.

37 I know that ye are Abraham's seed; but ye seek to kill me, because my word hath no place in you.

38 I speak that which I have seen with my Father: and ye do that which ye have seen with your father.

39 They answered and said unto him, Abraham is our father. Jesus saith unto them, If ye were Abraham's children, ye would do the works of Abraham.

40 But now ye seek to kill me, a man that hath told you the truth, which I have heard of God: this did not Abraham.

41 Ye do the deeds of your father. Then said they to him, We be not born of fornication; we have one Father, even God.

42 Jesus said unto them, If God were your Father, ye would love me: for I proceeded forth and came from God; neither came I of myself, but he sent me.

43 Why do ye not understand my speech? even because ye cannot hear my word.

44 Ye are of your father the devil, and the lusts of your father ye will do. He was a murderer from the beginning, and abode not in the truth, because there is no truth in him. When he speaketh a lie, he speaketh of his own: for he is a liar, and the father of it.

45 And because I tell you the truth, ye believe me not.

46 Which of you convinceth me of sin? And if I say the truth, why do ye not believe me?

47 He that is of God heareth God's words: ye therefore hear them not, because ye are not of God.

48 Then answered the Jews, and said unto him, Say we not well that thou art a Samaritan, and hast a devil?

49 Jesus answered, I have not a devil; but I honour my Father, and ye do dishonour me.

50 And I seek not mine own glory: there is one that seeketh and judgeth.

51 Verily, verily, I say unto you, If a man keep my saying, he shall never see death.

52 Then said the Jews unto him, Now we know that thou hast a devil. Abraham is dead, and the prophets; and thou sayest, If a man keep my saying, he shall never taste of death.

53 Art thou greater than our father Abraham, which is dead? and the prophets are dead: whom makest thou thyself?

54 Jesus answered, If I honour myself, my honour is nothing: it is my Father that honoureth me; of whom ye say, that he is your God:

55 Yet ye have not known him; but I know him: and if I should say, I know him not, I shall be a liar like unto you: but I know him, and keep his saying.

56 Your father Abraham rejoiced to see my day: and he saw it, and was glad.

57 Then said the Jews unto him, Thou art not yet fifty years old, and hast thou seen Abraham?

58 Jesus said unto them, Verily, verily, I say unto you, Before Abraham was, I am.

59 Then took they up stones to cast at him: but Jesus hid himself, and went out of the temple, going through the midst of them, and so passed by.

By not understanding his spiritual context, the message of Jesus does not seem to make much sense to those in the crowd. They cannot grasp that without the reconciliation brought about by Christ they are outside the kingdom of God. Jesus makes one of his most blunt statements concerning his deity in this passage: his Father is their God (verse 54), and he is the "I AM" of Exodus 3:14 (verse 58). The crowd immediately understood the implications of those statements, and picked up rocks to stone him for blasphemy. They completely got it then: Jesus identified himself to have equality with God, and to be God.

CHAPTER 9

1 And as Jesus passed by, he saw a man which was blind from his birth.
2 And his disciples asked him, saying, Master, who did sin, this man, or his parents, that he was born blind?
3 Jesus answered, Neither hath this man sinned, nor his parents: but that the works of God should be made manifest in him.
4 I must work the works of him that sent me, while it is day: the night cometh, when no man can work.
5 As long as I am in the world, I am the light of the world.
6 When he had thus spoken, he spat on the ground, and made clay of the spittle, and he anointed the eyes of the blind man with the clay,
7 And said unto him, Go, wash in the pool of Siloam, (which is by interpretation, Sent.) He went his way therefore, and washed, and came seeing.

Jesus demonstrated two things in this scene. One, he corrected an error that was widely held in his day (and unfortunately persists in some form today): that physical illness is the result of personal sin. The disciples asked what was a logical question. Since the man was *born* blind, they reasoned, was his blindness the result of *his* sin, or his *parent's* sin before his birth? Jesus straightened the disciples out. Birth defects and physical deformities are not the result of sin but are a consequence of our physical existence.

The second thing Jesus demonstrated was his authority over sickness and disease, which is one of the evidences that he is the Messiah. Jesus also exercised his kingly prerogative by healing the man in a unique way, which befits the situation. Jesus could have just spoken and the blind man could have had sight. But instead Jesus made a paste that the blind man would have to wash out in order to see. This was a test of the blind man's faith, and also set the stage for the events in the remainder of the chapter.

> *8 The neighbours therefore, and they which before had seen him that he was blind, said, Is not this he that sat and begged?*
> *9 Some said, This is he: others said, He is like him: but he said, I am he.*
> *10 Therefore said they unto him, How were thine eyes opened?*
> *11 He answered and said, A man that is called Jesus made clay, and anointed mine eyes, and said unto me, Go to the pool of Siloam, and wash: and I went and washed, and I received sight.*
> *12 Then said they unto him, Where is he? He said, I know not.*
> *13 They brought to the Pharisees him that aforetime was blind.*
> *14 And it was the sabbath day when Jesus made the clay, and opened his eyes.*

Jesus healing the blind man created an immediate response. The formerly blind man's friends and neighbors could not believe it. They hardly recognized him as a seeing person. This miracle of course caught the attention of the religious leaders. They once again were very unhappy with Jesus because he performed a miracle on the Sabbath, which they considered a violation of their laws and traditions.

> *15 Then again the Pharisees also asked him how he had received his sight. He said unto them, He put clay upon mine eyes, and I washed, and do see.*
> *16 Therefore said some of the Pharisees, This man is not of God, because he keepeth not the sabbath day. Others said, How can a man that is a sinner do such miracles? And there was a division among them.*
> *17 They say unto the blind man again, What sayest thou of him, that he hath opened thine eyes? He said, He is a prophet.*
> *18 But the Jews did not believe concerning him, that he had been blind, and received his sight, until they called the parents of him that had received his sight.*

19 And they asked them, saying, Is this your son, who ye say was born blind? how then doth he now see?

20 His parents answered them and said, We know that this is our son, and that he was born blind:

21 But by what means he now seeth, we know not; or who hath opened his eyes, we know not: he is of age; ask him: he shall speak for himself.

22 These words spake his parents, because they feared the Jews: for the Jews had agreed already, that if any man did confess that he was Christ, he should be put out of the synagogue.

23 Therefore said his parents, He is of age; ask him.

24 Then again called they the man that was blind, and said unto him, Give God the praise: we know that this man is a sinner.

25 He answered and said, Whether he be a sinner or no, I know not: one thing I know, that, whereas I was blind, now I see.

26 Then said they to him again, What did he to thee? how opened he thine eyes?

27 He answered them, I have told you already, and ye did not hear: wherefore would ye hear it again? will ye also be his disciples?

The Pharisee leaders had a big problem with this miracle. Something did happen and they could not deny it. Their problem was that the miracle happened on the Sabbath. Anything done on the Sabbath, according to their reasoning, could not be of God because obviously someone of God would keep their rules about the Sabbath! So instead of accepting the possibility that a true miracle took place, they started looking for a naturalistic explanation.

The blind man reasoned differently. Even though he had not seen Jesus, he believed based on the miracle itself. He was ready to follow Jesus literally "sight unseen." The blind man did not need anymore proof—he had faith.

28 Then they reviled him, and said, Thou art his disciple; but we are Moses' disciples.

29 We know that God spake unto Moses: as for this fellow, we know not from whence he is.

30 The man answered and said unto them, Why herein is a marvellous thing, that ye know not from whence he is, and yet he hath opened mine eyes.
31 Now we know that God heareth not sinners: but if any man be a worshipper of God, and doeth his will, him he heareth.
32 Since the world began was it not heard that any man opened the eyes of one that was born blind.
33 If this man were not of God, he could do nothing.

I have always found it amazing that the blind man, just a regular person and not having the benefit of theological training or schooling, understood exactly who Jesus was and where he came from. The formerly blind man realized the significance of the miracle: it pointed to divine authority in the one who performed it. The religious leaders, on the other hand, tried everything they knew so they could disprove the miracle. It seems like they already decided they would not believe anything that came from Jesus regardless of what may have happened.

34 They answered and said unto him, Thou wast altogether born in sins, and dost thou teach us? And they cast him out.
35 Jesus heard that they had cast him out; and when he had found him, he said unto him, Dost thou believe on the Son of God?
36 He answered and said, Who is he, Lord, that I might believe on him?
37 And Jesus said unto him, Thou hast both seen him, and it is he that talketh with thee.
38 And he said, Lord, I believe. And he worshipped him.
39 And Jesus said, For judgment I am come into this world, that they which see not might see; and that they which see might be made blind.
40 And some of the Pharisees which were with him heard these words, and said unto him, Are we blind also?
41 Jesus said unto them, If ye were blind, ye should have no sin: but now ye say, We see; therefore your sin remaineth.

The decision to follow Jesus sometimes comes with a price. The blind man experienced the cost of being Jesus' disciple because after his public statements about Jesus, he was cast out of the synagogue. Being "cast out" did not mean he was simply escorted to the door and asked to leave. It also meant that he was excommunicated from his religion and his culture. He could no longer worship in the synagogues or take part in his society. But he did not care. He knew what had happened to him, and believed.

After all this, Jesus came to the blind man. Once he learned that it was Jesus who healed him, he openly confessed that Jesus is God, and worshiped him as God. Jesus demonstrated that he is God by accepting the worship of the man, worship that is due only to God.

CHAPTER 10

1 Verily, verily, I say unto you, He that entereth not by the door into the sheepfold, but climbeth up some other way, the same is a thief and a robber.
2 But he that entereth in by the door is the shepherd of the sheep.
3 To him the porter openeth; and the sheep hear his voice: and he calleth his own sheep by name, and leadeth them out.
4 And when he putteth forth his own sheep, he goeth before them, and the sheep follow him: for they know his voice.
5 And a stranger will they not follow, but will flee from him: for they know not the voice of strangers.
6 This parable spake Jesus unto them: but they understood not what things they were which he spake unto them.
7 Then said Jesus unto them again, Verily, verily, I say unto you, I am the door of the sheep.
8 All that ever came before me are thieves and robbers: but the sheep did not hear them.
9 I am the door: by me if any man enter in, he shall be saved, and shall go in and out, and find pasture.
10 The thief cometh not, but for to steal, and to kill, and to destroy: I am come that they might have life, and that they might have it more abundantly.

In this chapter Jesus begins teaching the people using the imagery of sheep and the pastoral setting. The intended audience would understand his word pictures because many of them were from farms and rural lives themselves. Just because Jesus used imagery they were familiar with does not mean that they completely understood, however. Jesus was speaking to them in parables—stories that have deeper meanings. Like we learned in Chapter Eight, the key to understanding the teachings is to understand Jesus' context. Jesus was not teaching about sheep and farms. He was revealing attributes about *himself.* Jesus is the door, or the only way in. (Jesus will expand on this idea very plainly later in Chapter Fourteen, verse 6, where it states: "Jesus saith unto him, I am the way, the truth, and the life: no man cometh unto the Father, but by me.") Jesus is the shepherd, and the sheep of his flock know his voice. This unfortunately implies that if a sheep did not recognize his voice then it was not one of his. As John explains, the majority in the crowd did not recognize his voice.

11 I am the good shepherd: the good shepherd giveth his life for the sheep.

12 But he that is an hireling, and not the shepherd, whose own the sheep are not, seeth the wolf coming, and leaveth the sheep, and fleeth: and the wolf catcheth them, and scattereth the sheep.

13 The hireling fleeth, because he is an hireling, and careth not for the sheep.

14 I am the good shepherd, and know my sheep, and am known of mine.

15 As the Father knoweth me, even so know I the Father: and I lay down my life for the sheep.

16 And other sheep I have, which are not of this fold: them also I must bring, and they shall hear my voice; and there shall be one fold, and one shepherd.

17 Therefore doth my Father love me, because I lay down my life, that I might take it again.

18 No man taketh it from me, but I lay it down of myself. I have power to lay it down, and I have power to take it again. This commandment have I received of my Father.

Jesus continues teaching the crowd using parables that reflect the pastoral and rural life they readily understood. His teachings also continue to show how he is their Messiah and God. "The Good Shepherd" is a reference to Psalm 23, where it is stated that "The LORD *is* my shepherd." Jesus, the Good Shepherd, is the LORD of Israel.

As God, he has unique power and authority. Jesus reveals part of this power and authority by stating that he will intentionally allow himself to die, and then equally intentionally raise himself up from the dead. This is exactly what happened on Good Friday and Easter Sunday. Power over life and death is an ability reserved for deity alone.

19 There was a division therefore again among the Jews for these sayings.
20 And many of them said, He hath a devil, and is mad; why hear ye him?
21 Others said, These are not the words of him that hath a devil. Can a devil open the eyes of the blind?
22 And it was at Jerusalem the feast of the dedication, and it was winter.
23 And Jesus walked in the temple in Solomon's porch.
24 Then came the Jews round about him, and said unto him, How long dost thou make us to doubt? If thou be the Christ, tell us plainly.
25 Jesus answered them, I told you, and ye believed not: the works that I do in my Father's name, they bear witness of me.
26 But ye believe not, because ye are not of my sheep, as I said unto you.

The parables about the sheep and shepherd were not just random stories. The author John was setting the stage for this dramatic encounter. The religious leaders confronted Jesus in the temple and demanded to know if he was the Messiah or not. Jesus' reply was that he did tell them—over and over again, actually—through words and through the miracles he was performing. They were his credentials proving he was the Messiah and Son of God. They did not see the obvious clues because they were not his sheep, just like Jesus explained in the parables.

27 My sheep hear my voice, and I know them, and they follow me:
28 And I give unto them eternal life; and they shall never perish, neither shall any man pluck them out of my hand.
29 My Father, which gave them me, is greater than all; and no man is able to pluck them out of my Father's hand.
30 I and my Father are one.

I do not think that Jesus could have been much plainer than his statement in verse 30. He claimed complete equality with God. To those who say that Jesus never admitted he was God or deity, this is one of the verses that proves them absolutely wrong. Jesus DID claim to be God. It is intellectually dishonest to state that he did not. The author John knew for a fact that Jesus said he was God because he had heard it from his own lips.

31 Then the Jews took up stones again to stone him.
32 Jesus answered them, Many good works have I shewed you from my Father; for which of those works do ye stone me?
33 The Jews answered him, saying, For a good work we stone thee not; but for blasphemy; and because that thou, being a man, makest thyself God.
34 Jesus answered them, Is it not written in your law, I said, Ye are gods?
35 If he called them gods, unto whom the word of God came, and the scripture cannot be broken;
36 Say ye of him, whom the Father hath sanctified, and sent into the world, Thou blasphemest; because I said, I am the Son of God?
37 If I do not the works of my Father, believe me not.
38 But if I do, though ye believe not me, believe the works: that ye may know, and believe, that the Father is in me, and I in him.

The religious leaders understood precisely what Jesus meant. Jesus' statement probably caused uproar. Jesus then used their own legalistic logic system against them, showing the fallacy in their thinking and trying to point out the truth of his statement based on the works he did. Unfortunately, his attempts were futile.

39 Therefore they sought again to take him: but he escaped out of their hand,
40 And went away again beyond Jordan into the place where John at first baptized; and there he abode.
41 And many resorted unto him, and said, John did no miracle: but all things that John spake of this man were true.
42 And many believed on him there.

The religious leaders were beyond convincing, so Jesus escaped from them and left Jerusalem, returning to the rural parts of the country. As an interesting contrast, while the religious leaders rejected Jesus because they did not hear his voice, the "regular people" did hear his voice just like in the parables of the sheep. Those who believed in the countryside weighed the evidence and made their decision. They heard the Shepherd's voice calling them.

CHAPTER 11

1 Now a certain man was sick, named Lazarus, of Bethany, the town of Mary and her sister Martha.
2 (It was that Mary which anointed the Lord with ointment, and wiped his feet with her hair, whose brother Lazarus was sick.)
3 Therefore his sisters sent unto him, saying, Lord, behold, he whom thou lovest is sick.
4 When Jesus heard that, he said, This sickness is not unto death, but for the glory of God, that the Son of God might be glorified thereby.

The stage is being set for one of Jesus' greatest miracles. Lazarus and Jesus were very close friends. To Lazarus' sisters it seemed only natural to ask Jesus for his healing. They all believed in him and were well acquainted with his ability to heal. Jesus, however, was more than merely a healer, and saw Lazarus' sickness as an avenue that would bring glory to God, and further demonstrate his credentials as the Messiah and Son of God.

5 Now Jesus loved Martha, and her sister, and Lazarus.
6 When he had heard therefore that he was sick, he abode two days still in the same place where he was.
7 Then after that saith he to his disciples, Let us go into Judaea again.
8 His disciples say unto him, Master, the Jews of late sought to stone thee; and goest thou thither again?
9 Jesus answered, Are there not twelve hours in the day? If any man walk in the day, he stumbleth not, because he seeth the light of this world.

10 But if a man walk in the night, he stumbleth, because there is no light in him.

11 These things said he: and after that he saith unto them, Our friend Lazarus sleepeth; but I go, that I may awake him out of sleep.

12 Then said his disciples, Lord, if he sleep, he shall do well.

13 Howbeit Jesus spake of his death: but they thought that he had spoken of taking of rest in sleep.

14 Then said Jesus unto them plainly, Lazarus is dead.

15 And I am glad for your sakes that I was not there, to the intent ye may believe; nevertheless let us go unto him.

16 Then said Thomas, which is called Didymus, unto his fellow disciples, Let us also go, that we may die with him.

Jesus told his disciples that it was time to go to Judea and to conclude the situation with Lazarus. They were surprised. The disciples were worried about their safety, reasoning that it would be dangerous for them to go back to Judea. Jesus was not concerned about his safety, because he knew he was safe in the protection of his Father. He instead focused on Lazarus, and on doing a mighty work that would glorify God and further prove his Messiahship.

17 Then when Jesus came, he found that he had lain in the grave four days already.

18 Now Bethany was nigh unto Jerusalem, about fifteen furlongs off:

19 And many of the Jews came to Martha and Mary, to comfort them concerning their brother.

20 Then Martha, as soon as she heard that Jesus was coming, went and met him: but Mary sat still in the house.

21 Then said Martha unto Jesus, Lord, if thou hadst been here, my brother had not died.

22 But I know, that even now, whatsoever thou wilt ask of God, God will give it thee.

23 Jesus saith unto her, Thy brother shall rise again.

24 Martha saith unto him, I know that he shall rise again in the resurrection at the last day.

25 Jesus said unto her, I am the resurrection, and the life: he that believeth in me, though he were dead, yet shall he live:

26 And whosoever liveth and believeth in me shall never die. Believest thou this?
27 She saith unto him, Yea, Lord: I believe that thou art the Christ, the Son of God, which should come into the world.

When Jesus did arrive at the home of Mary and Martha, he stopped away from the main house, possibly in order to not bring attention to himself. Martha came out to meet Jesus where he was, and appears to question Jesus about why he did not come sooner. She was very aware of his power over sickness; she could not understand why Jesus did not come and heal one of his closest friends.

Jesus did not correct Martha about her very human feelings due to grief. Instead, he gently re-oriented the situation, bringing the focus back to glorifying God and showing his credentials as Messiah. Martha understood this and affirmed that she believed that Jesus is the Messiah and God.

28 And when she had so said, she went her way, and called Mary her sister secretly, saying, The Master is come, and calleth for thee.
29 As soon as she heard that, she arose quickly, and came unto him.
30 Now Jesus was not yet come into the town, but was in that place where Martha met him.
31 The Jews then which were with her in the house, and comforted her, when they saw Mary, that she rose up hastily and went out, followed her, saying, She goeth unto the grave to weep there.
32 Then when Mary was come where Jesus was, and saw him, she fell down at his feet, saying unto him, Lord, if thou hadst been here, my brother had not died.
33 When Jesus therefore saw her weeping, and the Jews also weeping which came with her, he groaned in the spirit, and was troubled,
34 And said, Where have ye laid him? They said unto him, Lord, come and see.
35 Jesus wept.
36 Then said the Jews, Behold how he loved him!
37 And some of them said, Could not this man, which opened the eyes of the blind, have caused that even this man should not have died?

38 Jesus therefore again groaning in himself cometh to the grave. It was a cave, and a stone lay upon it.

39 Jesus said, Take ye away the stone. Martha, the sister of him that was dead, saith unto him, Lord, by this time he stinketh: for he hath been dead four days.

40 Jesus saith unto her, Said I not unto thee, that, if thou wouldest believe, thou shouldest see the glory of God?

41 Then they took away the stone from the place where the dead was laid. And Jesus lifted up his eyes, and said, Father, I thank thee that thou hast heard me.

42 And I knew that thou hearest me always: but because of the people which stand by I said it, that they may believe that thou hast sent me.

43 And when he thus had spoken, he cried with a loud voice, Lazarus, come forth.

44 And he that was dead came forth, bound hand and foot with graveclothes: and his face was bound about with a napkin. Jesus saith unto them, Loose him, and let him go.

45 Then many of the Jews which came to Mary, and had seen the things which Jesus did, believed on him.

By raising Lazarus from the dead Jesus absolutely showed that he was deity. Only deity has power over life and death. The circumstances of this miracle make it difficult to explain it away by natural means. Lazarus was officially pronounced dead, and was in his tomb for four days. The decay process must have already started, as Martha believed in verse 39. Jesus raised Lazarus from the dead and returned him to his family healthy and without decay. This was no magician's trick. Only God could do this.

46 But some of them went their ways to the Pharisees, and told them what things Jesus had done.

47 Then gathered the chief priests and the Pharisees a council, and said, What do we? for this man doeth many miracles.

48 If we let him thus alone, all men will believe on him: and the Romans shall come and take away both our place and nation.

49 And one of them, named Caiaphas, being the high priest that same year, said unto them, Ye know nothing at all,

50 Nor consider that it is expedient for us, that one man should die for the people, and that the whole nation perish not.
51 And this spake he not of himself: but being high priest that year, he prophesied that Jesus should die for that nation;
52 And not for that nation only, but that also he should gather together in one the children of God that were scattered abroad.
53 Then from that day forth they took counsel together for to put him to death.

This is the way the world reacts to the truth of the Bible. In spite of overwhelming evidence people would rather reject it and keep things as they are, even if their status quo is a spiritual error.

This was also the response of most of the religious leaders. These men had the proof of Jesus' divinity and his fulfillment of the scriptures pointing to his being the Messiah. Instead of accepting him they were worried about the political situation and their power in the government. They did not deny Jesus' miracles or credentials. They rejected him for other reasons.

54 Jesus therefore walked no more openly among the Jews; but went thence unto a country near to the wilderness, into a city called Ephraim, and there continued with his disciples.
55 And the Jews' passover was nigh at hand: and many went out of the country up to Jerusalem before the passover, to purify themselves.
56 Then sought they for Jesus, and spake among themselves, as they stood in the temple, What think ye, that he will not come to the feast?
57 Now both the chief priests and the Pharisees had given a commandment, that, if any man knew where he were, he should shew it, that they might take him.

CHAPTER 12

1 Then Jesus six days before the passover came to Bethany, where Lazarus was which had been dead, whom he raised from the dead.

2 There they made him a supper; and Martha served: but Lazarus was one of them that sat at the table with him.

3 Then took Mary a pound of ointment of spikenard, very costly, and anointed the feet of Jesus, and wiped his feet with her hair: and the house was filled with the odour of the ointment.

4 Then saith one of his disciples, Judas Iscariot, Simon's son, which should betray him,

5 Why was not this ointment sold for three hundred pence, and given to the poor?

6 This he said, not that he cared for the poor; but because he was a thief, and had the bag, and bare what was put therein.

7 Then said Jesus, Let her alone: against the day of my burying hath she kept this.

8 For the poor always ye have with you; but me ye have not always.

Jesus considered Mary's anointing of his feet as preparation for his burial. Jesus always knew what his mission as Messiah was. Here his remarks are prophetic of his soon coming death and resurrection. He stated that he would not always be with us physically here on earth, which is a prediction of his future glorification.

9 Much people of the Jews therefore knew that he was there: and they came not for Jesus' sake only, but that they might see Lazarus also, whom he had raised from the dead.

10 But the chief priests consulted that they might put Lazarus also to death;

11 Because that by reason of him many of the Jews went away, and believed on Jesus.

The raising of Lazarus was a powerful miracle that confirmed Jesus' credentials as the Messiah. Notice that it is not just word of mouth for proof that Jesus is Messiah. People could come see Lazarus, and have concrete evidence that he had been raised, because he was standing right there! Not only were there eyewitnesses of this event but there was the recipient of it, too. The raising of Lazarus was a very powerful testimony for Jesus' Godship. It was so powerful that the religious leaders started to realize they would have to kill Lazarus as well as Jesus in order to stop people from believing on him.

12 On the next day much people that were come to the feast, when they heard that Jesus was coming to Jerusalem,

13 Took branches of palm trees, and went forth to meet him, and cried, Hosanna: Blessed is the King of Israel that cometh in the name of the Lord.

14 And Jesus, when he had found a young ass, sat thereon; as it is written,

15 Fear not, daughter of Sion; behold, thy King cometh, sitting on an ass's colt.

16 These things understood not his disciples at the first: but when Jesus was glorified, then remembered they that these things were written of him, and that they had done these things unto him.

17 The people therefore that was with him when he called Lazarus out of his grave, and raised him from the dead, bare record.

18 For this cause the people also met him, for that they heard that he had done this miracle.

19 The Pharisees therefore said among themselves, Perceive ye how ye prevail nothing? behold, the world is gone after him.

This passage is most often referred to as the Triumphal Entry. Jesus fulfills the specific prediction of Zechariah 9:9 of the entry of the King of the Jews into his city, which states:

Rejoice greatly, O daughter of Zion; shout, O daughter of Jerusalem: behold, thy King cometh unto thee: he is just, and having salvation; lowly, and riding upon an ass, and upon a colt the foal of an ass.

The proclamations by the people that Jesus was their King were not surprising. The people had heard that Jesus raised Lazarus from the dead, and many of them were eyewitnesses to this miracle.

20 And there were certain Greeks among them that came up to worship at the feast:
21 The same came therefore to Philip, which was of Bethsaida of Galilee, and desired him, saying, Sir, we would see Jesus.
22 Philip cometh and telleth Andrew: and again Andrew and Philip tell Jesus.
23 And Jesus answered them, saying, The hour is come, that the Son of man should be glorified.
24 Verily, verily, I say unto you, Except a corn of wheat fall into the ground and die, it abideth alone: but if it die, it bringeth forth much fruit.
25 He that loveth his life shall lose it; and he that hateth his life in this world shall keep it unto life eternal.
26 If any man serve me, let him follow me; and where I am, there shall also my servant be: if any man serve me, him will my Father honour.
27 Now is my soul troubled; and what shall I say? Father, save me from this hour: but for this cause came I unto this hour.
28 Father, glorify thy name. Then came there a voice from heaven, saying, I have both glorified it, and will glorify it again.

Jesus was not a reluctant prophet who made enemies and managed to get himself killed. He was on a mission. Jesus knew that his death was coming soon, and he predicted it. The human side of him seemed to have a concern but he was in absolute obedience to the Father, who himself provided witness.

29 The people therefore, that stood by, and heard it, said that it thundered: others said, An angel spake to him.

30 Jesus answered and said, This voice came not because of me, but for your sakes.
31 Now is the judgment of this world: now shall the prince of this world be cast out.
32 And I, if I be lifted up from the earth, will draw all men unto me.
33 This he said, signifying what death he should die.

Jesus' crucifixion was prophesied by him, and prophesied in other places in the Bible, such as Psalm 22. The usual way of capital punishment under Jewish law was by stoning. Under the Roman occupation the Jews were denied this option by Roman legal constraints. The Jewish leaders were forbidden from executing anyone. Only the Roman government could perform capital punishment, and they usually did so by crucifixion. This small detail of history was the reason why Jesus would be crucified.

34 The people answered him, We have heard out of the law that Christ abideth for ever: and how sayest thou, The Son of man must be lifted up? who is this Son of man?
35 Then Jesus said unto them, Yet a little while is the light with you. Walk while ye have the light, lest darkness come upon you: for he that walketh in darkness knoweth not whither he goeth.
36 While ye have light, believe in the light, that ye may be the children of light. These things spake Jesus, and departed, and did hide himself from them.
37 But though he had done so many miracles before them, yet they believed not on him:
38 That the saying of Esaias the prophet might be fulfilled, which he spake, Lord, who hath believed our report? and to whom hath the arm of the Lord been revealed?

These new revelations from Jesus were lost on the crowds. Their understanding of the Messiah was either very poor or did not include that he must suffer for the sins of humanity. Their confusion and unbelief was predicted by the prophet Isaiah in Chapter 53 verses 1-3 of his book:

Who hath believed our report? and to whom is the arm of the LORD revealed?
For he shall grow up before him as a tender plant, and as a root out of a dry ground: he hath no form nor comeliness; and when we shall see him, there is no beauty that we should desire him.
He is despised and rejected of men; a man of sorrows, and acquainted with grief: and we hid as it were our faces from him; he was despised, and we esteemed him not.

39 Therefore they could not believe, because that Esaias said again,
40 He hath blinded their eyes, and hardened their heart; that they should not see with their eyes, nor understand with their heart, and be converted, and I should heal them.
41 These things said Esaias, when he saw his glory, and spake of him.

The Prophet Isaiah, under the inspiration of God, was given a message for his time that continued to be applicable until Jesus' time. When Isaiah was called to be a prophet, God explained to him that the people would not understand, even though they saw and heard. Isaiah Chapter 6 verses 9 and 10 say:

And he said, Go, and tell this people, Hear ye indeed, but understand not; and see ye indeed, but perceive not.
Make the heart of this people fat, and make their ears heavy, and shut their eyes; lest they see with their eyes, and hear with their ears, and understand with their heart, and convert, and be healed.

42 Nevertheless among the chief rulers also many believed on him; but because of the Pharisees they did not confess him, lest they should be put out of the synagogue:
43 For they loved the praise of men more than the praise of God.
44 Jesus cried and said, He that believeth on me, believeth not on me, but on him that sent me.
45 And he that seeth me seeth him that sent me.
46 I am come a light into the world, that whosoever believeth on me should not abide in darkness.

*47 And if any man hear my words, and believe not, I judge him not:
for I came not to judge the world, but to save the world.*

*48 He that rejecteth me, and receiveth not my words, hath one that
judgeth him: the word that I have spoken, the same shall judge him in
the last day.*

*49 For I have not spoken of myself; but the Father which sent me,
he gave me a commandment, what I should say, and what I should
speak.*

*50 And I know that his commandment is life everlasting: whatsoever I
speak therefore, even as the Father said unto me, so I speak.*

Even though Jesus knew the end of his public ministry was coming
soon, he continued to teach the people and reveal himself to them.
Jesus was even clearer in this passage that he knew he was divinity.
Belief in him is the same as belief in the Father. Jesus took this concept
another step, explaining that to see him is the same as seeing God the
Father. There can be no doubt that in his teaching Jesus considered
himself to be God, and expressed it publicly.

Jesus also had some parting comments for those who had already
rejected him in spite of the evidence. Revealing what some of his
mission on earth entailed, Jesus explained that he came to bring light
to this dark world. This is exactly what he does as the Savior of the
world. He also revealed that on this mission he did not come to be a
judge of those who, while he was on the earth, rejected him. On the
last day, however, those who rejected him and his teachings will be
judged, and Jesus will sit in judgment over them. This will occur at his
Second Coming, when Jesus will sit as the Judge on the Great White
Throne (Revelation 20:11-15). The evidence that will convict these
men on that day will be the very words Jesus spoke in their hearing, the
words given them by the Father for their generation.

CHAPTER 13

1 Now before the feast of the passover, when Jesus knew that his hour was come that he should depart out of this world unto the Father, having loved his own which were in the world, he loved them unto the end.

2 And supper being ended, the devil having now put into the heart of Judas Iscariot, Simon's son, to betray him;

3 Jesus knowing that the Father had given all things into his hands, and that he was come from God, and went to God;

4 He riseth from supper, and laid aside his garments; and took a towel, and girded himself.

Chapter Thirteen chronicles some of the events of what we now call the Last Supper. Jesus was not acting arbitrarily. He knew his crucifixion and the redemption of mankind was happening soon. How could he know? Because he was God: he came from God, and was returning to him when these events were over. As God, Jesus was omniscient.

5 After that he poureth water into a bason, and began to wash the disciples' feet, and to wipe them with the towel wherewith he was girded.

6 Then cometh he to Simon Peter: and Peter saith unto him, Lord, dost thou wash my feet?

7 Jesus answered and said unto him, What I do thou knowest not now; but thou shalt know hereafter.

8 Peter saith unto him, Thou shalt never wash my feet. Jesus answered him, If I wash thee not, thou hast no part with me.

9 Simon Peter saith unto him, Lord, not my feet only, but also my hands and my head.

10 Jesus saith to him, He that is washed needeth not save to wash his feet, but is clean every whit: and ye are clean, but not all.

11 For he knew who should betray him; therefore said he, Ye are not all clean.

12 So after he had washed their feet, and had taken his garments, and was set down again, he said unto them, Know ye what I have done to you?

13 Ye call me Master and Lord: and ye say well; for so I am.

14 If I then, your Lord and Master, have washed your feet; ye also ought to wash one another's feet.

15 For I have given you an example, that ye should do as I have done to you.

16 Verily, verily, I say unto you, The servant is not greater than his lord; neither he that is sent greater than he that sent him.

17 If ye know these things, happy are ye if ye do them.

18 I speak not of you all: I know whom I have chosen: but that the scripture may be fulfilled, He that eateth bread with me hath lifted up his heel against me.

19 Now I tell you before it come, that, when it is come to pass, ye may believe that I am he.

Part of what Jesus did with the washing of the disciples' feet was to set a new example for them of how leadership was to be in his kingdom. But Jesus also continued to teach them who he was. Even as we get closer to the end, Jesus is still explaining to the disciples that they can absolutely believe he is God because of his fulfilled prophecies.

20 Verily, verily, I say unto you, He that receiveth whomsoever I send receiveth me; and he that receiveth me receiveth him that sent me.

21 When Jesus had thus said, he was troubled in spirit, and testified, and said, Verily, verily, I say unto you, that one of you shall betray me.

22 Then the disciples looked one on another, doubting of whom he spake.

23 Now there was leaning on Jesus' bosom one of his disciples, whom Jesus loved.

24 Simon Peter therefore beckoned to him, that he should ask who it should be of whom he spake.

25 He then lying on Jesus' breast saith unto him, Lord, who is it?

26 Jesus answered, He it is, to whom I shall give a sop, when I have dipped it. And when he had dipped the sop, he gave it to Judas Iscariot, the son of Simon.

27 And after the sop Satan entered into him. Then said Jesus unto him, That thou doest, do quickly.

28 Now no man at the table knew for what intent he spake this unto him.

29 For some of them thought, because Judas had the bag, that Jesus had said unto him, Buy those things that we have need of against the feast; or, that he should give something to the poor.

30 He then having received the sop went immediately out: and it was night.

The betrayal by Judas was not a surprise to Jesus. In his divine omniscience, he knew what events were coming. Judas' betrayal may have bothered Jesus in his human nature, but it was not a surprise.

31 Therefore, when he was gone out, Jesus said, Now is the Son of man glorified, and God is glorified in him.

32 If God be glorified in him, God shall also glorify him in himself, and shall straightway glorify him.

33 Little children, yet a little while I am with you. Ye shall seek me: and as I said unto the Jews, Whither I go, ye cannot come; so now I say to you.

34 A new commandment I give unto you, That ye love one another; as I have loved you, that ye also love one another.

35 By this shall all men know that ye are my disciples, if ye have love one to another.

36 Simon Peter said unto him, Lord, whither goest thou? Jesus answered him, Whither I go, thou canst not follow me now; but thou shalt follow me afterwards.

37 Peter said unto him, Lord, why cannot I follow thee now? I will lay down my life for thy sake.

38 Jesus answered him, Wilt thou lay down thy life for my sake? Verily, verily, I say unto thee, The cock shall not crow, till thou has denied me thrice.

Jesus knew that the sequence of events in the divine plan was now set in motion. The Son of man would be glorified, which would bring glory to God, who in turn would give glory to the Son. While this seems like a circular statement, it is really showing how Jesus receives the same glory as God, because he is God.

CHAPTER 14

1 Let not your heart be troubled: ye believe in God, believe also in me.
2 In my Father's house are many mansions: if it were not so, I would have told you. I go to prepare a place for you.
3 And if I go and prepare a place for you, I will come again, and receive you unto myself; that where I am, there ye may be also.
4 And whither I go ye know, and the way ye know.
5 Thomas saith unto him, Lord, we know not whither thou goest; and how can we know the way?
6 Jesus saith unto him, I am the way, the truth, and the life: no man cometh unto the Father, but by me.

This is a very clear statement by Jesus about who he is and his relationship with the Father. In Chapter Ten, Jesus began explaining this idea in a parable. For his disciples in private he states it plainly. In this chapter, Jesus again affirms his divinity by appealing to the disciples that the same faith that they have in God should be applied to him. As Jesus speaks of his soon return to the Father, and the plans he has for the disciples (and all future disciples), Thomas gets confused. Thomas does not think he knows where Jesus is talking about, but if he reflected on it, he would realize he did know. Jesus had been talking for months about his return to the Father. Jesus answered him using similar imagery that he used in Chapter Ten, where he taught that he was the door of the sheep. *The way* is him. Jesus is the door that must be passed through. He is the only way to God.

7 If ye had known me, ye should have known my Father also: and from henceforth ye know him, and have seen him.

8 Philip saith unto him, Lord, shew us the Father, and it sufficeth us.

9 Jesus saith unto him, Have I been so long time with you, and yet hast thou not known me, Philip? he that hath seen me hath seen the Father; and how sayest thou then, Shew us the Father?

10 Believest thou not that I am in the Father, and the Father in me? the words that I speak unto you I speak not of myself: but the Father that dwelleth in me, he doeth the works.

11 Believe me that I am in the Father, and the Father in me: or else believe me for the very works' sake.

Even though he is now speaking plainly to them, the disciples do not completely understand. Believers (and non-believers) throughout history have asked the same question, not realizing they already have the answer. We do not have to ask God to reveal himself to us, because he already has! *To see and know Jesus is to see and know God.* It really is that simple because, as he has been explaining all along, *Jesus is God.* While we should take Jesus at his word that he is one with the Father, his works are evidence enough to prove that it is true.

12 Verily, verily, I say unto you, He that believeth on me, the works that I do shall he do also; and greater works than these shall he do; because I go unto my Father.

13 And whatsoever ye shall ask in my name, that will I do, that the Father may be glorified in the Son.

14 If ye shall ask any thing in my name, I will do it.

15 If ye love me, keep my commandments.

16 And I will pray the Father, and he shall give you another Comforter, that he may abide with you for ever;

17 Even the Spirit of truth; whom the world cannot receive, because it seeth him not, neither knoweth him: but ye know him; for he dwelleth with you, and shall be in you.

Jesus here makes a prediction about the future indwelling of the Holy Spirit for each believer. This will be a fulfillment of Joel 2:28:

And it shall come to pass afterward that I will pour out My Spirit on all flesh; your sons and your daughters shall prophesy, your old men shall dream dreams, your young men shall see visions.

It is by the indwelling of the Holy Spirit that we have comfort and assurance, and we have the ability to operate in the spiritual realm ourselves.

18 I will not leave you comfortless: I will come to you.
19 Yet a little while, and the world seeth me no more; but ye see me: because I live, ye shall live also.
20 At that day ye shall know that I am in my Father, and ye in me, and I in you.
21 He that hath my commandments, and keepeth them, he it is that loveth me: and he that loveth me shall be loved of my Father, and I will love him, and will manifest myself to him.
22 Judas saith unto him, not Iscariot, Lord, how is it that thou wilt manifest thyself unto us, and not unto the world?
23 Jesus answered and said unto him, If a man love me, he will keep my words: and my Father will love him, and we will come unto him, and make our abode with him.
24 He that loveth me not keepeth not my sayings: and the word which ye hear is not mine, but the Father's which sent me.

In a slightly enigmatic statement, Jesus predicts the near future for the disciples and how their faith will grow because of what will happen. After Jesus rose from the dead, he did not reveal himself to the public, but only to his disciples. They will see him alive, and they will know that Jesus is in the Father, and that they have eternal life and a relationship with him and the Father. The other Judas thought it was odd that Jesus would not reveal himself to the public, but only to those who believe. This however is God's plan: that only those who believe Jesus' teachings will receive the grace of God to become his children.

25 These things have I spoken unto you, being yet present with you.

26 But the Comforter, which is the Holy Ghost, whom the Father will send in my name, he shall teach you all things, and bring all things to your remembrance, whatsoever I have said unto you.

27 Peace I leave with you, my peace I give unto you: not as the world giveth, give I unto you. Let not your heart be troubled, neither let it be afraid.

28 Ye have heard how I said unto you, I go away, and come again unto you. If ye loved me, ye would rejoice, because I said, I go unto the Father: for my Father is greater than I.

29 And now I have told you before it come to pass, that, when it is come to pass, ye might believe.

30 Hereafter I will not talk much with you: for the prince of this world cometh, and hath nothing in me.

31 But that the world may know that I love the Father; and as the Father gave me commandment, even so I do. Arise, let us go hence.

Jesus again predicts the coming of the Holy Spirit to indwell in each believer. The uniqueness of this prophecy is that the Holy Spirit will supernaturally teach them and sharpen their memory to remember his teachings. This is exactly what happens in the biblical concept of *inspiration*. Because of this supernatural inspiration of the disciples, we have the guarantee of accuracy of the documents we now call the New Testament.

CHAPTER 15

1 I am the true vine, and my Father is the husbandman.

2 Every branch in me that beareth not fruit he taketh away: and every branch that beareth fruit, he purgeth it, that it may bring forth more fruit.

3 Now ye are clean through the word which I have spoken unto you.

4 Abide in me, and I in you. As the branch cannot bear fruit of itself, except it abide in the vine; no more can ye, except ye abide in me.

5 I am the vine, ye are the branches: He that abideth in me, and I in him, the same bringeth forth much fruit: for without me ye can do nothing.

6 If a man abide not in me, he is cast forth as a branch, and is withered; and men gather them, and cast them into the fire, and they are burned.

7 If ye abide in me, and my words abide in you, ye shall ask what ye will, and it shall be done unto you.

8 Herein is my Father glorified, that ye bear much fruit; so shall ye be my disciples.

9 As the Father hath loved me, so have I loved you: continue ye in my love.

10 If ye keep my commandments, ye shall abide in my love; even as I have kept my Father's commandments, and abide in his love.

11 These things have I spoken unto you, that my joy might remain in you, and that your joy might be full.

12 This is my commandment, That ye love one another, as I have loved you.

13 Greater love hath no man than this, that a man lay down his life for his friends.

14 Ye are my friends, if ye do whatsoever I command you.

Jesus applies some familiar images to show the disciples how the new life they will experience in him will be. Using imagery of grapevines and vineyards, Jesus explains that he is the true vine, and the Father the husbandman (the farmer who tends to the vines and grapes) of the vineyard. This is a statement of the divinity of both he and the Father. Like a foreshadow of Paul's use of the grapevine and how we are grafted in to become children of God by adoption, Jesus uses the grapevine as an illustration of how we are part of the vine through him, and how we must abide in him for spiritual growth and life. "Abide" is a special word that carries the meaning of *remaining in close relationship*. It is also a word, when applied to relationships that is reserved for our relationship to God alone, as in Psalm 91:1:

> *He that dwelleth in the secret place of the most High shall abide under the shadow of the Almighty.*

For Jesus to now state that all are to abide in him, Jesus is taking on to himself attributes that belong to God alone.

15 Henceforth I call you not servants; for the servant knoweth not what his lord doeth: but I have called you friends; for all things that I have heard of my Father I have made known unto you.
16 Ye have not chosen me, but I have chosen you, and ordained you, that ye should go and bring forth fruit, and that your fruit should remain: that whatsoever ye shall ask of the Father in my name, he may give it you.
17 These things I command you, that ye love one another.
18 If the world hate you, ye know that it hated me before it hated you.
19 If ye were of the world, the world would love his own: but because ye are not of the world, but I have chosen you out of the world, therefore the world hateth you.
20 Remember the word that I said unto you, The servant is not greater than his lord. If they have persecuted me, they will also persecute you; if they have kept my saying, they will keep yours also.
21 But all these things will they do unto you for my name's sake, because they know not him that sent me.

22 If I had not come and spoken unto them, they had not had sin: but now they have no cloak for their sin.
23 He that hateth me hateth my Father also.

In this passage that prophecies about the persecution that will come to his followers, Jesus again emphasizes his deity to the disciples. By hating him, his enemies will also hate his Father, which implies that Father and Son are equal.

24 If I had not done among them the works which none other man did, they had not had sin: but now have they both seen and hated both me and my Father.
25 But this cometh to pass, that the word might be fulfilled that is written in their law, They hated me without a cause.
26 But when the Comforter is come, whom I will send unto you from the Father, even the Spirit of truth, which proceedeth from the Father, he shall testify of me:
27 And ye also shall bear witness, because ye have been with me from the beginning.

The theme in this part of the chapter is a familiar one: Jesus' works will point a reasonable person to the knowledge that he is the Messiah of Israel and the Son of God. Unfortunately, for the most part those of his time were not reasonable people. They would reject him and turn him over to be crucified.

CHAPTER 16

*1 These things have I spoken unto you, that ye should not be offended.
2 They shall put you out of the synagogues: yea, the time cometh, that whosoever killeth you will think that he doeth God service.
3 And these things will they do unto you, because they have not known the Father, nor me.
4 But these things have I told you, that when the time shall come, ye may remember that I told you of them. And these things I said not unto you at the beginning, because I was with you.
5 But now I go my way to him that sent me; and none of you asketh me, Whither goest thou?
6 But because I have said these things unto you, sorrow hath filled your heart.
7 Nevertheless I tell you the truth; It is expedient for you that I go away: for if I go not away, the Comforter will not come unto you; but if I depart, I will send him unto you.
8 And when he is come, he will reprove the world of sin, and of righteousness, and of judgment:
9 Of sin, because they believe not on me;
10 Of righteousness, because I go to my Father, and ye see me no more;
11 Of judgment, because the prince of this world is judged.*

In this passage, Jesus again speaks about returning to the Father and his pre-existent state. Jesus gave the disciples a warning about the future persecution they would encounter because of their faith in him. He also gave another promise of the coming of the Holy Spirit.

12 I have yet many things to say unto you, but ye cannot bear them now.
13 Howbeit when he, the Spirit of truth, is come, he will guide you into all truth: for he shall not speak of himself; but whatsoever he shall hear, that shall he speak: and he will shew you things to come.
14 He shall glorify me: for he shall receive of mine, and shall shew it unto you.
15 All things that the Father hath are mine: therefore said I, that he shall take of mine, and shall shew it unto you.
16 A little while, and ye shall not see me: and again, a little while, and ye shall see me, because I go to the Father.
17 Then said some of his disciples among themselves, What is this that he saith unto us, A little while, and ye shall not see me: and again, a little while, and ye shall see me: and, Because I go to the Father?
18 They said therefore, What is this that he saith, A little while? we cannot tell what he saith.

In his discourse with the disciples, Jesus predicts numerous times his death and resurrection. There is absolute confidence in his words that he will be resurrected and will see his disciples again physically. He knows this because he is God himself.

19 Now Jesus knew that they were desirous to ask him, and said unto them, Do ye enquire among yourselves of that I said, A little while, and ye shall not see me: and again, a little while, and ye shall see me?
20 Verily, verily, I say unto you, That ye shall weep and lament, but the world shall rejoice: and ye shall be sorrowful, but your sorrow shall be turned into joy.
21 A woman when she is in travail hath sorrow, because her hour is come: but as soon as she is delivered of the child, she remembereth no more the anguish, for joy that a man is born into the world.
22 And ye now therefore have sorrow: but I will see you again, and your heart shall rejoice, and your joy no man taketh from you.

Jesus knew what was on the disciples' minds as he predicted his coming death and resurrection. They wanted to ask questions, but were too afraid to ask. Jesus gave them an illustration to explain what they were about to go through: it would be like a woman going through childbirth. While the act of labor is painful, there is joy once the child is delivered. The disciples would be filled with grief when Jesus was crucified, but their sorrow would be turned to joy when they saw him after his resurrection.

23 And in that day ye shall ask me nothing. Verily, verily, I say unto you, Whatsoever ye shall ask the Father in my name, he will give it you.

24 Hitherto have ye asked nothing in my name: ask, and ye shall receive, that your joy may be full.

25 These things have I spoken unto you in proverbs: but the time cometh, when I shall no more speak unto you in proverbs, but I shall shew you plainly of the Father.

26 At that day ye shall ask in my name: and I say not unto you, that I will pray the Father for you:

27 For the Father himself loveth you, because ye have loved me, and have believed that I came out from God.

28 I came forth from the Father, and am come into the world: again, I leave the world, and go to the Father.

29 His disciples said unto him, Lo, now speakest thou plainly, and speakest no proverb.

30 Now are we sure that thou knowest all things, and needest not that any man should ask thee: by this we believe that thou camest forth from God.

31 Jesus answered them, Do ye now believe?

32 Behold, the hour cometh, yea, is now come, that ye shall be scattered, every man to his own, and shall leave me alone: and yet I am not alone, because the Father is with me.

33 These things I have spoken unto you, that in me ye might have peace. In the world ye shall have tribulation: but be of good cheer; I have overcome the world.

In this excerpt, Jesus again emphasizes to his disciples how he is deity. He plainly states to them that he came from the Father (God), and was returning to him. The disciples reinforced and testified to this idea of Jesus being deity by affirming that they, too, believed that Jesus was from God.

CHAPTER 17

1 These words spake Jesus, and lifted up his eyes to heaven, and said, Father, the hour is come; glorify thy Son, that thy Son also may glorify thee:
2 As thou hast given him power over all flesh, that he should give eternal life to as many as thou hast given him.
3 And this is life eternal, that they might know thee the only true God, and Jesus Christ, whom thou hast sent.
4 I have glorified thee on the earth: I have finished the work which thou gavest me to do.
5 And now, O Father, glorify thou me with thine own self with the glory which I had with thee before the world was.

Chapter Seventeen is a lengthy prayer of Jesus to his Father concerning his disciples and future believers. In this prayer, he gives statements, like in verse five, pronouncing his deity and pre-existence.

6 I have manifested thy name unto the men which thou gavest me out of the world: thine they were, and thou gavest them me; and they have kept thy word.
7 Now they have known that all things whatsoever thou hast given me are of thee.
8 For I have given unto them the words which thou gavest me; and they have received them, and have known surely that I came out from thee, and they have believed that thou didst send me.

This set of verses again affirms Jesus' divinity and relationship with the Father. Interestingly, Jesus also mentions that the disciples understand that he came from the Father, and is on a mission from him.

> *9 I pray for them: I pray not for the world, but for them which thou hast given me; for they are thine.*
> *10 And all mine are thine, and thine are mine; and I am glorified in them.*
> *11 And now I am no more in the world, but these are in the world, and I come to thee. Holy Father, keep through thine own name those whom thou hast given me, that they may be one, as we are.*

Verse eleven is a clear statement of Jesus' divinity. Jesus plainly states that he and the Father are one and equal.

> *12 While I was with them in the world, I kept them in thy name: those that thou gavest me I have kept, and none of them is lost, but the son of perdition; that the scripture might be fulfilled.*
> *13 And now come I to thee; and these things I speak in the world, that they might have my joy fulfilled in themselves.*
> *14 I have given them thy word; and the world hath hated them, because they are not of the world, even as I am not of the world.*
> *15 I pray not that thou shouldest take them out of the world, but that thou shouldest keep them from the evil.*
> *16 They are not of the world, even as I am not of the world.*
> *17 Sanctify them through thy truth: thy word is truth.*
> *18 As thou hast sent me into the world, even so have I also sent them into the world.*
> *19 And for their sakes I sanctify myself, that they also might be sanctified through the truth.*
> *20 Neither pray I for these alone, but for them also which shall believe on me through their word;*
> *21 That they all may be one; as thou, Father, art in me, and I in thee, that they also may be one in us: that the world may believe that thou hast sent me.*

22 And the glory which thou gavest me I have given them; that they may be one, even as we are one:

23 I in them, and thou in me, that they may be made perfect in one; and that the world may know that thou hast sent me, and hast loved them, as thou hast loved me.

24 Father, I will that they also, whom thou hast given me, be with me where I am; that they may behold my glory, which thou hast given me: for thou lovedst me before the foundation of the world.

25 O righteous Father, the world hath not known thee: but I have known thee, and these have known that thou hast sent me.

26 And I have declared unto them thy name, and will declare it: that the love wherewith thou hast loved me may be in them, and I in them.

In this lengthy passage, Jesus reveals in his prayer that his origin is supernatural. He is not of this world, but was sent here by the Father for a specific purpose. Jesus was in and with the Father before the creation of the earth (verse 24), and has the glory given him by the Father.

CHAPTER 18

1 When Jesus had spoken these words, he went forth with his disciples over the brook Cedron, where was a garden, into the which he entered, and his disciples.
2 And Judas also, which betrayed him, knew the place: for Jesus ofttimes resorted thither with his disciples.
3 Judas then, having received a band of men and officers from the chief priests and Pharisees, cometh thither with lanterns and torches and weapons.
4 Jesus therefore, knowing all things that should come upon him, went forth, and said unto them, Whom seek ye?
5 They answered him, Jesus of Nazareth. Jesus saith unto them, I am he. And Judas also, which betrayed him, stood with them.
6 As soon then as he had said unto them, I am he, they went backward, and fell to the ground.

Right after praying, Jesus was confronted by an armed group sent there to arrest him. Jesus was not surprised by their arrival, because in his omniscience he knew what was going to happen. While this and the following incidents appear at first glance to show Jesus at his weakest point, it really shows him at his strongest. Throughout the entire trial process, Jesus is self-controlled and peaceful in spirit. He is fully aware of who he is, and why he is doing what he is doing. That he possessed as the Jamieson-Fausset-Brown Commentary called "majesty" is apparent as the group fell down simply because of the personal power Jesus possessed.

7 Then asked he them again, Whom seek ye? And they said, Jesus of Nazareth.
8 Jesus answered, I have told you that I am he: if therefore ye seek me, let these go their way:
9 That the saying might be fulfilled, which he spake, Of them which thou gavest me have I lost none.

This is the fulfillment of the prophecy Jesus made in his prayer in Chapter Seventeen, verse 12. None of the original twelve apostles were arrested or killed, except for Judas who would later commit suicide.

10 Then Simon Peter having a sword drew it, and smote the high priest's servant, and cut off his right ear. The servant's name was Malchus.
11 Then said Jesus unto Peter, Put up thy sword into the sheath: the cup which my Father hath given me, shall I not drink it?

Jesus was fully aware of his mission to be the Savior of the world. Even though Peter meant well, Jesus would have none of it. His kingdom would not be set up by force or be of this world. He would not have his Father's will thwarted by the actions of men.

12 Then the band and the captain and officers of the Jews took Jesus, and bound him,
13 And led him away to Annas first; for he was father in law to Caiaphas, which was the high priest that same year.
14 Now Caiaphas was he, which gave counsel to the Jews, that it was expedient that one man should die for the people.

Jesus continued to show that he was in control in spite of the chaos around his arrest. He told his arresters to let the disciples go (which they did) and healed the man who's ear was cut off. Nothing happened to Jesus that he did not allow. He allowed himself to be captured and he allowed himself to be bound because he knew he was doing the Father's will. Jesus voluntarily went to the cross to pay for our sins.

The reference to Caiaphas making a prophecy about Jesus is interesting. God can use even those who do not believe in his plan. This has happened several times in Scripture. Habbakuk reveals how God was using a heathen nation to punish Israel, even though that nation did not believe in him and was not aware that they were being used. The same thing appears to be the case with Caiaphas. He really did not believe the message or mission of Jesus. In spite of his unbelief, God used him in his office of high priest to deliver yet another confirmation of what Jesus' mission was.

15 And Simon Peter followed Jesus, and so did another disciple: that disciple was known unto the high priest, and went in with Jesus into the palace of the high priest.

16 But Peter stood at the door without. Then went out that other disciple, which was known unto the high priest, and spake unto her that kept the door, and brought in Peter.

17 Then saith the damsel that kept the door unto Peter, Art not thou also one of this man's disciples? He saith, I am not.

18 And the servants and officers stood there, who had made a fire of coals; for it was cold: and they warmed themselves: and Peter stood with them, and warmed himself.

19 The high priest then asked Jesus of his disciples, and of his doctrine.

20 Jesus answered him, I spake openly to the world; I ever taught in the synagogue, and in the temple, whither the Jews always resort; and in secret have I said nothing.

21 Why askest thou me? ask them which heard me, what I have said unto them: behold, they know what I said.

22 And when he had thus spoken, one of the officers which stood by struck Jesus with the palm of his hand, saying, Answerest thou the high priest so?

23 Jesus answered him, If I have spoken evil, bear witness of the evil: but if well, why smitest thou me?

24 Now Annas had sent him bound unto Caiaphas the high priest.

Jesus appears to be rather insulting to Annas, but I think he is actually being consistent. The religious leaders had three years of evidence that Jesus was the Messiah. Jesus presented his credentials; all the people who heard him speak and who saw him perform miracles knew that. At this point all the religious leaders needed to do was ask the people who were witnesses of it.

25 And Simon Peter stood and warmed himself. They said therefore unto him, Art not thou also one of his disciples? He denied it, and said, I am not.
26 One of the servants of the high priest, being his kinsman whose ear Peter cut off, saith, Did not I see thee in the garden with him?
27 Peter then denied again: and immediately the cock crew.

The denial of Jesus by Peter is a very well known part of the narrative. Jesus showed his omniscience by predicting that Peter would do this exact thing. (Look back to Chapter Thirteen, verse 38. Peter was pretty bold about all the brave things he would do, but Jesus knew better, because he had all knowledge of what was to come.)

28 Then led they Jesus from Caiaphas unto the hall of judgment: and it was early; and they themselves went not into the judgment hall, lest they should be defiled; but that they might eat the passover.
29 Pilate then went out unto them, and said, What accusation bring ye against this man?
30 They answered and said unto him, If he were not a malefactor, we would not have delivered him up unto thee.
31 Then said Pilate unto them, Take ye him, and judge him according to your law. The Jews therefore said unto him, It is not lawful for us to put any man to death:
32 That the saying of Jesus might be fulfilled, which he spake, signifying what death he should die.

Jesus prophesied earlier in his ministry that he must be lifted up, which is a reference to crucifixion. (Look back to Chapter Twelve, verses 32 and 33.) This is the beginning of the fulfillment of that prophesy.

33 Then Pilate entered into the judgment hall again, and called Jesus, and said unto him, Art thou the King of the Jews?

34 Jesus answered him, Sayest thou this thing of thyself, or did others tell it thee of me?

35 Pilate answered, Am I a Jew? Thine own nation and the chief priests have delivered thee unto me: what hast thou done?

36 Jesus answered, My kingdom is not of this world: if my kingdom were of this world, then would my servants fight, that I should not be delivered to the Jews: but now is my kingdom not from hence.

37 Pilate therefore said unto him, Art thou a king then? Jesus answered, Thou sayest that I am a king. To this end was I born, and for this cause came I into the world, that I should bear witness unto the truth. Every one that is of the truth heareth my voice.

38 Pilate saith unto him, What is truth? And when he had said this, he went out again unto the Jews, and saith unto them, I find in him no fault at all.

39 But ye have a custom, that I should release unto you one at the passover: will ye therefore that I release unto you the King of the Jews?

40 Then cried they all again, saying, Not this man, but Barabbas. Now Barabbas was a robber.

In this conversation with Pilate, Jesus answers Pilate's questions by affirming that he is the King of the Jews. The language used in the conversation does not register to our modern ears because it sounds so passive, but Jesus is telling Pilate he is King, not only of the Jews, but supernaturally also. His kingdom *is not of this world*. The Messiah of the Jews is not just King of the Jewish nation, but also a spiritual Savior and King over all creation, both natural and supernatural.

CHAPTER 19

1 Then Pilate therefore took Jesus, and scourged him.
2 And the soldiers platted a crown of thorns, and put it on his head, and they put on him a purple robe,
3 And said, Hail, King of the Jews! and they smote him with their hands.
4 Pilate therefore went forth again, and saith unto them, Behold, I bring him forth to you, that ye may know that I find no fault in him.
5 Then came Jesus forth, wearing the crown of thorns, and the purple robe. And Pilate saith unto them, Behold the man!
6 When the chief priests therefore and officers saw him, they cried out, saying, Crucify him, crucify him. Pilate saith unto them, Take ye him, and crucify him: for I find no fault in him.
7 The Jews answered him, We have a law, and by our law he ought to die, because he made himself the Son of God.

The actions of the soldiers were most likely a cruel joke. They put a purple robe (color of royalty) on Jesus, and a crown of thorns on his head. They were mocking him instead of acknowledging that Jesus was King of the Jews. The words of the Jewish leaders, on the other hand, are not in mockery. They testify here to Pilate that Jesus did indeed claim to be the Son of God and deity.

8 When Pilate therefore heard that saying, he was the more afraid;
9 And went again into the judgment hall, and saith unto Jesus, Whence art thou? But Jesus gave him no answer.

10 Then saith Pilate unto him, Speakest thou not unto me? knowest thou not that I have power to crucify thee, and have power to release thee?

11 Jesus answered, Thou couldest have no power at all against me, except it were given thee from above: therefore he that delivered me unto thee hath the greater sin.

Pilate has his doubts about all this. Whether he personally believed that Jesus was the King of the Jews and Messiah is not clear. What we can know from these passages, and the other gospel records, is that Pilate understood that this was no normal case. He did understand that Jesus was unique, and may have thought that he was being brought before him out of political and religious jealousy.

12 And from thenceforth Pilate sought to release him: but the Jews cried out, saying, If thou let this man go, thou art not Caesar's friend: whosoever maketh himself a king speaketh against Caesar.

13 When Pilate therefore heard that saying, he brought Jesus forth, and sat down in the judgment seat in a place that is called the Pavement, but in the Hebrew, Gabbatha.

14 And it was the preparation of the passover, and about the sixth hour: and he saith unto the Jews, Behold your King!

15 But they cried out, Away with him, away with him, crucify him. Pilate saith unto them, Shall I crucify your King? The chief priests answered, We have no king but Caesar.

16 Then delivered he him therefore unto them to be crucified. And they took Jesus, and led him away.

What I have always found fascinating in these passages is the difference in attitudes between the crowds and religious leaders and Pilate. I think Pilate really did believe that Jesus was a true king of some kind. Pilate may have realized that Jesus was being delivered to him because of an internal religious power struggle. Unfortunately, no amount of logic or persuasion was possible at this point. Mob mentality was taking over, which took away most of Pilate's options.

17 And he bearing his cross went forth into a place called the place of a skull, which is called in the Hebrew Golgotha:
18 Where they crucified him, and two other with him, on either side one, and Jesus in the midst.
19 And Pilate wrote a title, and put it on the cross. And the writing was, JESUS OF NAZARETH THE KING OF THE JEWS.
20 This title then read many of the Jews: for the place where Jesus was crucified was nigh to the city: and it was written in Hebrew, and Greek, and Latin.
21 Then said the chief priests of the Jews to Pilate, Write not, The King of the Jews; but that he said, I am King of the Jews.
22 Pilate answered, What I have written I have written.

Pilate really wanted to release Jesus because he realized that he did nothing criminally wrong to deserve to be executed. With the mob frenzy and other pressures working against him, Pilate was forced to pass judgment in order to keep the peace. But he did manage to get the last word in. Pilate displayed for all to see that Jesus is the King of the Jews. The religious leaders did not like that. They challenged what Pilate wrote, but he refused to change a thing.

23 Then the soldiers, when they had crucified Jesus, took his garments, and made four parts, to every soldier a part; and also his coat: now the coat was without seam, woven from the top throughout.
24 They said therefore among themselves, Let us not rend it, but cast lots for it, whose it shall be: that the scripture might be fulfilled, which saith, They parted my raiment among them, and for my vesture they did cast lots. These things therefore the soldiers did.

This part of the passage is a fulfillment of the prophecy in Psalm 22:

For dogs have compassed me: the assembly of the wicked have inclosed me: they pierced my hands and my feet.
I may tell all my bones: they look and stare upon me.
They part my garments among them, and cast lots upon my vesture.

Fulfillment of prophecy is an important evidence of the claim to be the Messiah. In order to be the Messiah, these prophetic events have to happen exactly as foretold. It can be argued that because it is possible to know what the prophecies are, then it could be possible to fake fulfillment. However, this fulfillment was while Jesus was hanging on the cross. He could not possibly influence what the Roman soldiers were doing with his clothes while he was hanging there.

25 Now there stood by the cross of Jesus his mother, and his mother's sister, Mary the wife of Cleophas, and Mary Magdalene.
26 When Jesus therefore saw his mother, and the disciple standing by, whom he loved, he saith unto his mother, Woman, behold thy son!
27 Then saith he to the disciple, Behold thy mother! And from that hour that disciple took her unto his own home.
28 After this, Jesus knowing that all things were now accomplished, that the scripture might be fulfilled, saith, I thirst.
29 Now there was set a vessel full of vinegar: and they filled a spunge with vinegar, and put it upon hyssop, and put it to his mouth.
30 When Jesus therefore had received the vinegar, he said, It is finished: and he bowed his head, and gave up the ghost.

Jesus did something on the cross that no other human being has ever done. Jesus had complete control over his own life and death. Just as he predicted, no one could take his life from him. He gave up his life only when he decided that all was fulfilled for the redemption of mankind.

31 The Jews therefore, because it was the preparation, that the bodies should not remain upon the cross on the sabbath day, (for that sabbath day was an high day,) besought Pilate that their legs might be broken, and that they might be taken away.
32 Then came the soldiers, and brake the legs of the first, and of the other which was crucified with him.
33 But when they came to Jesus, and saw that he was dead already, they brake not his legs:

34 But one of the soldiers with a spear pierced his side, and forthwith came there out blood and water.

35 And he that saw it bare record, and his record is true: and he knoweth that he saith true, that ye might believe.

36 For these things were done, that the scripture should be fulfilled, A bone of him shall not be broken.

37 And again another scripture saith, They shall look on him whom they pierced.

Once again Scripture is being fulfilled, and Jesus has no possible way to influence its outcome. The religious leaders did not like the idea of leaving dying people out during the holy day, so they asked the Romans to do something about it. The Roman practice was to break the legs of those being executed to hasten their demise. To the soldiers' surprise Jesus was already dead. Just to make sure, one of them thrust Jesus through the side with his spear, and saw the evidence they needed. Both of these actions, according to John the author, were in fulfillment of Psalm 34:20 and Zechariah 12:10.

38 And after this Joseph of Arimathaea, being a disciple of Jesus, but secretly for fear of the Jews, besought Pilate that he might take away the body of Jesus: and Pilate gave him leave. He came therefore, and took the body of Jesus.

39 And there came also Nicodemus, which at the first came to Jesus by night, and brought a mixture of myrrh and aloes, about an hundred pound weight.

40 Then took they the body of Jesus, and wound it in linen clothes with the spices, as the manner of the Jews is to bury.

41 Now in the place where he was crucified there was a garden; and in the garden a new sepulchre, wherein was never man yet laid.

42 There laid they Jesus therefore because of the Jews' preparation day; for the sepulchre was nigh at hand.

After Jesus' death he was taken down from the cross and his body was prepared for burial. Nicodemus, the Jewish leader who came to see Jesus by night in Chapter Three, took care of all of the arrangements. Jesus was buried nearby in a new, never used tomb. These activities fulfilled specific prophesies concerning the Messiah, as found in Isaiah Chapter 53, verses 9 and 12. These verses in Isaiah predict that the Messiah will be killed with criminals, but will be buried with the wealthy, specifically a rich man's grave. This is exactly what happened with Jesus.

CHAPTER 20

1 The first day of the week cometh Mary Magdalene early, when it was yet dark, unto the sepulchre, and seeth the stone taken away from the sepulchre.

All the disciples, including Mary Magdalene, absolutely believed that Jesus was dead. The idea that he could come back from the dead was very foreign to them. They had seen people die before and they knew that when a person was dead they were gone for good. Unfortunately, they forgot Jesus' teachings on how he would be raised on the third day.

2 Then she runneth, and cometh to Simon Peter, and to the other disciple, whom Jesus loved, and saith unto them, They have taken away the Lord out of the sepulchre, and we know not where they have laid him.
3 Peter therefore went forth, and that other disciple, and came to the sepulchre.
4 So they ran both together: and the other disciple did outrun Peter, and came first to the sepulchre.
5 And he stooping down, and looking in, saw the linen clothes lying; yet went he not in.
6 Then cometh Simon Peter following him, and went into the sepulchre, and seeth the linen clothes lie,
7 And the napkin, that was about his head, not lying with the linen clothes, but wrapped together in a place by itself.

8 Then went in also that other disciple, which came first to the sepulchre, and he saw, and believed.
9 For as yet they knew not the scripture, that he must rise again from the dead.
10 Then the disciples went away again unto their own home.

Mary ran back to where they were staying and told Peter and John what she witnessed. These two disciples then went to the tomb themselves and found it empty. Here we have three individuals giving eyewitness testimony: that tomb was *empty*.

11 But Mary stood without at the sepulchre weeping: and as she wept, she stooped down, and looked into the sepulchre,
12 And seeth two angels in white sitting, the one at the head, and the other at the feet, where the body of Jesus had lain.
13 And they say unto her, Woman, why weepest thou? She saith unto them, Because they have taken away my Lord, and I know not where they have laid him.
14 And when she had thus said, she turned herself back, and saw Jesus standing, and knew not that it was Jesus.
15 Jesus saith unto her, Woman, why weepest thou? whom seekest thou? She, supposing him to be the gardener, saith unto him, Sir, if thou have borne him hence, tell me where thou hast laid him, and I will take him away.
16 Jesus saith unto her, Mary. She turned herself, and saith unto him, Rabboni; which is to say, Master.
17 Jesus saith unto her, Touch me not; for I am not yet ascended to my Father: but go to my brethren, and say unto them, I ascend unto my Father, and your Father; and to my God, and your God.
18 Mary Magdalene came and told the disciples that she had seen the Lord, and that he had spoken these things unto her.

Mary was very upset about the fact that the body of Jesus was missing. While the men went back home, she stayed. Her sorrow produced tears so heavy that she was blinded. When the risen Jesus came to her she thought he was the gardener. It was only seeing Jesus in his resurrected state that she received relief.

19 Then the same day at evening, being the first day of the week, when the doors were shut where the disciples were assembled for fear of the Jews, came Jesus and stood in the midst, and saith unto them, Peace be unto you.
20 And when he had so said, he shewed unto them his hands and his side. Then were the disciples glad, when they saw the Lord.

Jesus suspends the rules of nature by simply appearing in the midst of the disciples. He exercises his kingship and authority over matter and our time/space continuum. While this is obviously a spiritual manifestation, he also presents to the disciples his hands and side, which positively identifies him as being physically alive.

21 Then said Jesus to them again, Peace be unto you: as my Father hath sent me, even so send I you.
22 And when he had said this, he breathed on them, and saith unto them, Receive ye the Holy Ghost:
23 Whose soever sins ye remit, they are remitted unto them; and whose soever sins ye retain, they are retained.

Jesus exercised his authority as deity by conferring onto the disciples the Holy Spirit. Jesus also exercises another part of his divinity by delegating to the disciples the ability to declare sins forgiven. Only God himself can forgive sins, and only God can delegate forgiveness of sins to others.

24 But Thomas, one of the twelve, called Didymus, was not with them when Jesus came.
25 The other disciples therefore said unto him, We have seen the Lord. But he said unto them, Except I shall see in his hands the print of the nails, and put my finger into the print of the nails, and thrust my hand into his side, I will not believe.
26 And after eight days again his disciples were within, and Thomas with them: then came Jesus, the doors being shut, and stood in the midst, and said, Peace be unto you.

27 Then saith he to Thomas, Reach hither thy finger, and behold my hands; and reach hither thy hand, and thrust it into my side: and be not faithless, but believing.
28 And Thomas answered and said unto him, My Lord and my God.
29 Jesus saith unto him, Thomas, because thou hast seen me, thou hast believed: blessed are they that have not seen, and yet have believed.
30 And many other signs truly did Jesus in the presence of his disciples, which are not written in this book:
31 But these are written, that ye might believe that Jesus is the Christ, the Son of God; and that believing ye might have life through his name.

Thomas is often called "the doubter" because of the things he said, but I think that is a mis-characterization. The other disciples had already seen Jesus. All Thomas wants is the same proof the others' already saw (Jesus demonstrated in verse 20 the exact things Thomas asked to see). Thomas shows some pride by doing a "one-up" on the others: he does not want to just see like the others, but he wants to touch in order to have proof. When Jesus returns to visit the disciples, in a display of his omniscience he uses Thomas' exact words against him. Thomas knows he has been rebuked and acknowledges that Jesus is God. What I think is interesting is that there is no record of Thomas actually putting his fingers in Jesus' hands or side. Thomas was humbled by this experience and apparently did not need any physical proof.

CHAPTER 21

1 After these things Jesus shewed himself again to the disciples at the sea of Tiberias; and on this wise shewed he himself.

2 There were together Simon Peter, and Thomas called Didymus, and Nathanael of Cana in Galilee, and the sons of Zebedee, and two other of his disciples.

3 Simon Peter saith unto them, I go a fishing. They say unto him, We also go with thee. They went forth, and entered into a ship immediately: and that night they caught nothing.

4 But when the morning was now come, Jesus stood on the shore: but the disciples knew not that it was Jesus.

5 Then Jesus saith unto them, Children, have ye any meat? They answered him, No.

6 And he said unto them, Cast the net on the right side of the ship, and ye shall find. They cast therefore, and now they were not able to draw it for the multitude of fishes.

7 Therefore that disciple whom Jesus loved saith unto Peter, It is the Lord. Now when Simon Peter heard that it was the Lord, he girt his fisher's coat unto him, (for he was naked,) and did cast himself into the sea.

8 And the other disciples came in a little ship; (for they were not far from land, but as it were two hundred cubits,) dragging the net with fishes.

9 As soon then as they were come to land, they saw a fire of coals there, and fish laid thereon, and bread.

10 Jesus saith unto them, Bring of the fish which ye have now caught.

11 Simon Peter went up, and drew the net to land full of great fishes, an hundred and fifty and three: and for all there were so many, yet was not the net broken.

John recalls here his eyewitness testimony of seeing Jesus following his resurrection. After a period of waiting, Peter decides to go back to work fishing and some of the other disciples decide to go with him. What occurs after this is an encounter with the risen Christ. Jesus calls out to them from the shore but they do not recognize him or his voice. Jesus has no intention of hiding from them. Giving a command to fish from the right side of the boat (presumably the opposite side from what they were using), Jesus creates a situation that recalls his calling of the disciples in Luke 5:4-11. That incident was a miracle specifically to show Peter that Jesus was the Messiah. Both John and Peter made this connection and realized that the man on the shore was Jesus. Peter's emotion and devotion was so great that he jumped into the sea and swam to shore, not waiting for the boat to land so he could see him.

12 Jesus saith unto them, Come and dine. And none of the disciples durst ask him, Who art thou? knowing that it was the Lord.

13 Jesus then cometh, and taketh bread, and giveth them, and fish likewise.

14 This is now the third time that Jesus shewed himself to his disciples, after that he was risen from the dead.

15 So when they had dined, Jesus saith to Simon Peter, Simon, son of Jonas, lovest thou me more than these? He saith unto him, Yea, Lord; thou knowest that I love thee. He saith unto him, Feed my lambs.

16 He saith to him again the second time, Simon, son of Jonas, lovest thou me? He saith unto him, Yea, Lord; thou knowest that I love thee. He saith unto him, Feed my sheep.

17 He saith unto him the third time, Simon, son of Jonas, lovest thou me? Peter was grieved because he said unto him the third time, Lovest thou me? And he said unto him, Lord, thou knowest all things; thou knowest that I love thee. Jesus saith unto him, Feed my sheep.

18 Verily, verily, I say unto thee, When thou wast young, thou girdedst thyself, and walkedst whither thou wouldest: but when thou shalt be old, thou shalt stretch forth thy hands, and another shall gird thee, and carry thee whither thou wouldest not.

19 This spake he, signifying by what death he should glorify God. And when he had spoken this, he saith unto him, Follow me.

Jesus restores Peter's relationship with him after Peter's denial before the crucifixion. Even in this personal moment, Jesus shows his omniscience by revealing to Peter his future martyrdom for the faith.

20 Then Peter, turning about, seeth the disciple whom Jesus loved following; which also leaned on his breast at supper, and said, Lord, which is he that betrayeth thee?

21 Peter seeing him saith to Jesus, Lord, and what shall this man do?

22 Jesus saith unto him, If I will that he tarry till I come, what is that to thee? follow thou me.

23 Then went this saying abroad among the brethren, that that disciple should not die: yet Jesus said not unto him, He shall not die; but, If I will that he tarry till I come, what is that to thee?

24 This is the disciple which testifieth of these things, and wrote these things: and we know that his testimony is true.

25 And there are also many other things which Jesus did, the which, if they should be written every one, I suppose that even the world itself could not contain the books that should be written. Amen.

This chapter and the book conclude with John's identification of himself as an eyewitness and as the author of this book. Jesus gave many proofs and evidences of his divinity and that he is the Messiah. John asserts that Jesus gave so much proof that the world could not hold all the books that could be written about it! John should know, because he was there.

This assertion silences many claims of contradictions between the different gospel accounts. John did not mention the incidents he refers to from Luke because it was not necessary. It was already recorded by someone else. As it is, John is satisfied with the details he has given so that future readers would conclude, like he did, that Jesus is God and the Savior of the world.

ABOUT THE AUTHOR

DOCTOR JON F. DEWEY is a former Senior Noncommissioned Officer in the United States Army. He served in numerous assignments in the United States and overseas, including tours in Germany, Korea, and Hawaii.

Dr. Dewey has served local churches as an interim pastor, pastor of adults, worship leader, music minister and teacher. He is the author of the book *Before You Marry—A Guidebook for Engaged Couples*, as well as numerous magazine and newspaper articles.

His academic achievements include a Bachelor of Biblical Studies degree, a Master of Ministry degree, and a Doctor of Ministry degree from Bethany Bible College and Theological Seminary, Dothan, Alabama. He also holds a Bachelor of Science in Sociology degree and a Master of Science in Behavioral Science degree from Cameron University, Lawton, Oklahoma.